FINE-TUNING HUGGING FACE FOR SOFTWARE DEVELOPERS

The Essential Guide to Building Smarter Software by Conquering LLMs

Written By
CHRIS C. THOMPSON

Table of Contents

Level Up Your Dev Game with Fine-tuned LLMs

Imagine a coding world where machines not only understand your code, but actively help you write it, navigate it, and even document it with ease. Sounds like science fiction, right? Well, hold onto your hard drives, because that future is closer than you think, and the key to unlocking it lies in a powerful technique called **fine-tuning large language models (LLMs)**.

But what exactly are LLMs, and how can fine-tuning them make you a coding rockstar?

Think of LLMs as super-powered language processors trained on massive amounts of text data. They can generate text, translate languages, write different kinds of creative content, and even answer your questions in an informative way. It's like having a super-smart language assistant on steroids, except it's specifically designed for the world of code.

Now, fine-tuning takes these pre-trained LLMs and tailors them to your specific needs. It's like teaching your language assistant to speak fluent developer, enabling it to understand your code's intricacies and assist you in amazing ways.

Imagine generating code snippets based on your descriptions, effortlessly searching through mountains of code, or automatically creating crystal-clear documentation – all with the help of your fine-tuned LLM sidekick.

But wait, there's more! Fine-tuning isn't just about cool tricks. It's about **boosting your productivity, efficiency, and overall coding power**. It's about saying goodbye to repetitive tasks and hello to a world where you can focus on the truly creative and challenging aspects of software development.

Intrigued? We thought so! This book is your roadmap to becoming a fine-tuning master, unlocking the potential of LLMs to transform your coding journey. We'll guide you through every step, from understanding the fundamentals to putting your newfound skills into practice with real-world projects.

Ready to ditch the mundane and embrace the future of coding? Buckle up, developer, and let's embark on this fine-tuning adventure together!

We value your feedback and would love to hear your thoughts on this book! Please leave a review and rating to share your experience.

Part 1: Foundations of Fine-tuning for Developers

CHAPTER 1

Demystifying Large Language Models (LLMs) - Your New Coding Besties

Hold onto your syntax highlighters, because we're about to dive into the fascinating world of large language models (LLMs). Forget R2-D2, these are the coding companions you've actually been dreaming of! But before we unleash their powers, let's crack open the hood and see what makes them tick.

1.1. What are LLMs and how do they work?

Large language models (LLMs) are powerful AI models trained on massive amounts of text data. This data could include code, books, articles, or even social media posts. By analyzing these vast amounts of text, LLMs learn to understand and process language in complex ways.

Here's how they work:

1. Neural networks: Imagine a network of interconnected nodes, similar to the human brain. LLMs use such networks, where each node processes information and passes it on to others.

2. Learning from data: As LLMs are exposed to massive amounts of text, they identify patterns and relationships between words. This allows them to understand the meaning and context of language.

3. Processing and generating text: Based on the learned patterns, LLMs can:

- **Understand your questions and requests:** When you ask an LLM something, it uses its knowledge to find relevant information and provide an answer.
- **Generate text:** Give an LLM a prompt or description, and it can write code snippets, comments, or even documentation.
- **Translate languages:** LLMs can translate code or text from one language to another, breaking down communication barriers.

It's important to remember that LLMs are still under development, and their capabilities vary depending on the specific model and training data. However, they offer exciting potential for developers looking to automate tasks, improve productivity, and gain new insights from code.

In the next section, we'll explore different LLM architectures and their strengths for developers.

1.2. Key LLM Architectures: Transformers, LSTMs, and the Gang

Navigating the world of LLMs can feel like stepping onto a racetrack filled with high-performance engines, each boasting unique strengths and weaknesses. Choosing the right one for your development needs requires understanding these architectural nuances. Let's delve into two prominent contenders:

1. Transformers: The Speedy Grand Prix Racers

Imagine the lightning-fast reflexes of a Formula One champion – that's the essence of Transformers. Their secret lies in **parallel processing**, allowing them to analyze vast amounts of text simultaneously. This makes them shine at handling lengthy code sequences, effortlessly grasping the context of your entire project as you build.

Key terms to remember here are the **encoder-decoder architecture** and the **attention mechanism**. The encoder processes the input text, while the decoder translates it into the desired output (like generating code or translating between languages). The attention mechanism allows the model to focus on specific parts of the input text, crucial for understanding complex relationships within code.

So, why are Transformers ideal for developers? Their parallel processing prowess makes them perfect for tasks like code generation and translation, where handling long sequences is essential. Additionally, their ability to capture intricate relationships between words in code proves invaluable for tasks like code completion or suggesting relevant documentation. However, like any high-performance car, they come with their limitations. Training and running these models can be computationally expensive, and their inner workings might be less interpretable compared to other architectures.

2. LSTMs: The Reliable Endurance Runners

Think of LSTMs (Long Short-Term Memory) as the dependable marathons runners of the LLM world. They excel at **remembering information for extended periods**, making them champions for tasks requiring context awareness.

Key terms in this context are **gated recurrent units** and **memory cells**. These allow LSTMs to retain information over longer stretches, unlike traditional neural networks that tend to forget quickly.

For developers, this translates to several advantages. LSTMs excel at code completion tasks, where remembering past information is crucial. They're also adept at generating longer text formats like comments or documentation, where maintaining context throughout the content is important. And compared to Transformers, they generally require less computational power, making them more accessible for resource-constrained projects.

However, like any long-distance runner, LSTMs might not be the best choice for every sprint. They may struggle with exceptionally long code sequences compared to Transformers, and their processing speed can be slower due to the sequential nature of their architecture.

Ultimately, the best LLM architecture for you depends on the specific demands of your project. Consider factors like the task at hand (code generation, translation, etc.), the complexity and length of your code, and your available computational resources. Remember, choosing the right tool for the job is crucial for unlocking the full potential of LLMs in your development journey.

In the next section, we'll explore the exciting potential of LLMs for developers while acknowledging their current limitations, providing a balanced perspective on their impact in the coding world.

1.3. Strengths and Limitations of LLMs for Developers: A Practical View

Large language models (LLMs) have entered the developer's toolbox, offering exciting possibilities. Let's explore their strengths and limitations with real-world examples and code snippets to understand their true potential:

Strengths:

- **Automation:** Imagine writing basic comments, documentation snippets, or even test cases automatically! LLMs can analyze existing code and generate relevant comments, saving you time and effort. For example, an LLM trained on Python code could analyze a function and automatically generate a comment explaining its purpose:

Python

```python
def calculate_distance(x1, y1, x2, y2):

    """Calculates the Euclidean distance
between two points."""

    # ... existing code ...
```

- **Code Completion:** Stuck mid-thought while coding? LLMs can predict the next line of code based on your current context. This can be helpful for completing repetitive tasks or remembering forgotten syntax. For example, an LLM trained on Javascript might suggest closing quotes after you start a string:

JavaScript

```javascript
const message = "Hello, world!";
```

- **Code Search and Navigation:** Finding specific functions or variables in large codebases can be tedious. LLMs can understand the meaning of your search query and navigate complex code structures efficiently.

Imagine searching for "user authentication logic" within a vast codebase and getting relevant results highlighted.

-

- **Documentation Generation:** Manually writing comprehensive documentation can be time-consuming. LLMs can analyze your code and automatically generate documentation, saving you valuable time. For example, an LLM trained on API documentation could analyze your code and generate API reference sheets with descriptions, parameters, and usage examples.

-

Limitations:

- **Data Dependence:** LLMs are only as good as the data they are trained on. Biased or inaccurate data can lead to biased or inaccurate results. Be mindful of the data sources used to train the LLM you choose.
- **Limited Reasoning:** While LLMs can generate impressive text, they may not always understand the deeper meaning or logic behind it. Don't rely solely on LLMs for critical decision-making, always validate their suggestions.
- **Explainability:** Understanding how an LLM arrives at its output can be challenging. This lack of transparency can make it difficult to debug errors or trust their suggestions fully.
- **Computational Cost:** Training and running large LLMs can be computationally expensive. Consider your project's resource constraints before diving in.

Remember: LLMs are powerful tools, but they are not magic wands. Use them judiciously, understand their limitations, and focus on how they can augment your skills rather than replace them. With this balanced approach, LLMs can unlock new possibilities and boost your development efficiency.

In the next chapter, we'll explore the different types of LLMs available and how to choose the right one for your project, equipping you to start your fine-tuning journey!

CHAPTER 2

Unveiling Hugging Face: Your Gateway to LLM Superpowers

Remember those LLMs we met in the previous chapter? Well, imagine a platform that makes working with them as easy as ordering pizza online. Enter Hugging Face – your one-stop shop for accessing, exploring, and fine-tuning powerful LLMs for your developer needs. Buckle up, because we're about to unlock its secrets!

2.1. Exploring the Hugging Face Platform and Ecosystem: Your LLM Toolkit

Think of building with large language models (LLMs) like assembling a toolbox. You need the right tools for the job, and Hugging Face offers a comprehensive platform to equip you:

Pre-trained LLMs: Imagine a library stocked with specialized tools, each addressing different tasks. Hugging Face boasts hundreds of pre-trained models covering diverse areas like code generation, translation, and question answering. Here are some concrete examples to illustrate their capabilities:

- **Code generation:** Struggling to write repetitive boilerplate code or want to explore different implementation options? Models like Codex or GPT-J can generate code snippets based on your descriptions or comments, saving you time and effort. Imagine describing the functionality you need, and the LLM generating different potential code solutions for you to evaluate.

- **Translation:** Working on a multilingual project or need to understand code comments in another language? Models like m2m_transformer or Helsinki-NLP specialize in language translation. Imagine seamlessly translating code comments, documentation, or even entire codebases, breaking down language barriers and expanding your project's reach.

- **Question answering:** Stuck on a technical question about a specific library or API? Models like facebook/bart-base or allenai/roberta-base can answer your questions directly, drawing from their vast knowledge base of code and documentation. Imagine having an instant technical consultant at your fingertips, providing concise and informative answers to your coding queries.

Fine-tuning tools and resources: Don't settle for off-the-shelf tools. Hugging Face provides user-friendly libraries like transformers and datasets to fine-tune pre-trained models for your specific needs. This is like taking a general-purpose tool and customizing it to perfectly fit your project requirements. Imagine adjusting the parameters of a code generation model to specialize in a particular programming language or tailoring a question-answering model to your specific codebase terminology.

Vibrant community: Building with LLMs isn't a solo journey. Hugging Face fosters a thriving community through forums, discussions, and events. Connect with other developers, share experiences, learn from each other's successes and challenges, and get inspired by innovative LLM applications. Imagine collaborating with fellow enthusiasts, discussing best practices, troubleshooting issues together, and pushing the boundaries of what's possible with LLMs.

Beyond models and tools: Hugging Face offers more than just pre-trained models and fine-tuning tools:

- **Datasets:** Train your own LLMs from scratch or find inspiration from existing datasets covering various domains, like code repositories, question-answer pairs, or dialogue conversations. This is like having raw materials to fuel your LLM creations and experiment with different training approaches. Imagine using a dataset of real-world code examples to train a model for specific coding tasks or leveraging a question-answer dataset to build a more comprehensive technical knowledge base for your LLM.
- **Courses and workshops:** Level up your LLM skills with interactive learning materials designed for developers of all levels. This is like attending an LLM boot camp specifically tailored to your needs, boosting your expertise and confidence in working with these

powerful tools. Imagine learning best practices for fine-tuning, exploring advanced LLM architectures, and gaining insights from industry experts.

Remember, Hugging Face is a gateway, not a destination. It empowers you to explore, learn, and build with LLMs in a user-friendly and collaborative environment. With its diverse offerings and supportive community, Hugging Face can be your one-stop shop for unlocking the potential of LLMs in your development journey.

Next up, we'll explore the specific benefits of using Hugging Face for developers, highlighting how this platform can accelerate your coding workflow and enhance your development capabilities.

2.2. Why Hugging Face is Your Developer's Dream for LLMs

Imagine building with LLMs as smoothly as assembling IKEA furniture (minus the frustration, hopefully!). That's the beauty of Hugging Face – it empowers developers like you with numerous benefits:

1. Save Time and Resources:

- **Pre-trained models:** Forget building LLMs from scratch. Access hundreds of ready-to-use models, each a specialist in tasks like code generation, translation, or question answering. Think of it as having an expert team prepared for your project, saving you months of development time.

- **Fine-tuning tools:** No coding wizardry needed! Hugging Face provides user-friendly libraries like transformers and datasets to fine-tune pre-trained models for your specific project. Imagine easily adjusting a code generation LLM model to specialize in your preferred programming language, saving you the hassle of complex coding.

2. Focus on Your Specific Problem:

- Ditch the LLM intricacies and concentrate on what matters – your project! Use Hugging Face's tools to tailor pre-trained models to your unique needs. Think of it as having a team of experts working alongside you, understanding your project's nuances and delivering solutions aligned with your goals.
- **Real-world examples:** See Hugging Face in action! Explore their Space for projects showcasing diverse applications. Imagine finding inspiration for your own use case, like a model translating documentation or generating comments for specific code libraries.

3. Stay Ahead of the Curve:

- **Cutting-edge models:** Access the latest LLM advancements as they emerge. Hugging Face is constantly integrating new models and research, keeping you at the forefront of LLM technology. Think of it as having a direct line to the future of AI, ensuring your projects leverage the latest and most powerful tools.

- **Active community:** Learn from and collaborate with other developers passionate about LLMs. Engage in discussions, attend workshops, and stay informed about the latest trends. Think of it as having a vibrant support network, helping you overcome challenges and unlock the full potential of LLMs.

4. Concrete benefits, not just buzzwords:

Let's translate these benefits into real-world scenarios:

- **Scenario:** You're developing a multilingual app and need to translate code comments and documentation efficiently.
- **Hugging Face benefit:** Use a pre-trained translation model like m2m_transformer and fine-tune it with your specific code terminology, ensuring accurate and consistent translations within your project.
- **Scenario:** You're writing repetitive test cases and want to automate the process.
- **Hugging Face benefit:** Utilize a code generation model like Codex, fine-tuned on relevant test case examples, to automatically generate basic test cases, freeing up your time for more complex tasks.

Remember: Hugging Face is your launchpad, not your finish line. It empowers you to experiment, innovate, and push the boundaries of what's possible with LLMs. So, dive in, explore, and unleash your coding creativity!

In the next chapter, we'll delve into the exciting world of selecting the right LLM for your project, equipping you to embark on your fine-tuning journey and maximize the power of Hugging Face in your development endeavors!

2.3. Dive into Hugging Face: Setting Up Your Development Environment

Ready to unlock the potential of LLMs with Hugging Face? Let's roll up our sleeves and set up your development environment. It's easier than you think!

1. Prerequisites:

- **Python 3.6 or later:** Make sure you have Python installed. Check by running python --version in your terminal. If not, download it from https://www.python.org/downloads/.
- **Pip:** Pip is a package installer for Python. If you installed Python using the official website, pip should be included. You can check by running pip --version in your terminal. If not, download it from https://pip.pypa.io/en/stable/installation/.

2. Installing the Hugging Face library:

Open your terminal and run the following command:

Bash

```
pip install transformers datasets
```

This installs the two core libraries you'll need to interact with Hugging Face models and datasets.

3. Testing your setup:

Let's verify everything works! Run this code in your terminal:

Python

```python
from transformers import AutoTokenizer, AutoModelForSeq2SeqLM


tokenizer = AutoTokenizer.from_pretrained("facebook/bart-base")

model = AutoModelForSeq2SeqLM.from_pretrained("facebook/bart-base")


input_ids = tokenizer("Hello, world! How are you?", return_tensors="pt")

output = model(**input_ids)
```

```
decoded_text                              =
tokenizer.batch_decode(output.sequences,
skip_special_tokens=True)[0]


print(decoded_text)
```

If everything is set up correctly, you should see a response like "Hi! How are you doing?" generated by the model.

4. Exploring further:

Congratulations! You're now equipped to explore the vast world of Hugging Face. Remember, this is just the beginning:

- **Hugging Face Hub:** Browse pre-trained models, datasets, and code examples: https://huggingface.co/
- **Documentation:** Deep dive into the libraries and tools: [[invalid URL removed]]([invalid URL removed])
- **Tutorials:** Learn new skills and explore advanced concepts: [[invalid URL removed]]([invalid URL removed])

By setting up your environment and taking these first steps, you've opened the door to a world of possibilities with LLMs.

In the next chapter, we'll delve into the exciting world of choosing the right LLM for your project, empowering you to navigate the diverse options and make informed decisions for your development journey!

CHAPTER 3

Embarking on the Fine-tuning Adventure - Where LLMs Become Your Coding Besties

Remember those pre-trained LLMs we met in Chapter 2? Think of them as talented athletes, each with their strengths and specialties. But wouldn't it be amazing if you could train them specifically for your coding challenges, turning them into your personalized coding companions? That's the magic of fine-tuning! Buckle up, because we're diving into the heart of this powerful technique.

3.1. Fine-tuning LLMs: Unlocking Their Superpowers with Focused Training

Imagine you have a talented chef who can cook various cuisines. But what if you could train them to become a master of your grandma's secret lasagna recipe? That's the essence of fine-tuning large language models (LLMs)! We take a pre-trained LLM, already knowledgeable about language, and give it extra training focused on your specific coding tasks.

Here's how it works:

1. Transfer Learning: Building on Existing Knowledge:

Think of it like building a new floor on top of a sturdy foundation. LLMs are pre-trained on massive amounts of text, giving them a strong understanding of language patterns and relationships. Fine-tuning leverages this foundation, allowing you to focus on teaching the LLM the specifics of your domain.

Code Example:

Imagine you have a pre-trained LLM like Codex familiar with various programming languages and coding concepts. You want to fine-tune it to generate Python code specific to your project involving data manipulation. You would:

1. **Prepare a dataset:** Gather a collection of Python code snippets (preferably from your project) showcasing data manipulation tasks like reading from files, processing dataframes, and performing calculations.
2. **Fine-tuning process:** You wouldn't need to train the LLM from scratch on basic Python syntax or language understanding. Instead, you'd focus on fine-tuning the parameters related to code generation and data manipulation tasks.
3. **Result:** After fine-tuning, you could provide the LLM a natural language description like "Read data from a CSV file, filter based on specific criteria, and calculate the average value in a particular column." The LLM, leveraging its pre-trained knowledge and fine-tuned

understanding of data manipulation, could generate relevant Python code for this task.

2. Data is Key: Feeding the Right Ingredients:

Just like any good recipe needs the right ingredients, fine-tuning relies on high-quality data relevant to your task. This could be code examples, documentation, or even technical Q&A data. The more targeted and plentiful your data, the better the LLM will learn and adapt.

Code Example:

Let's say you want to fine-tune a code generation model to write comments for your Javascript code. You'd provide the model with a dataset of existing Javascript code paired with human-written comments that explain the purpose and functionality of different code blocks. During fine-tuning, the model would analyze these examples, learning the specific relationships between Javascript code patterns and the kind of comments that are helpful and informative.

3. Tuning the Knobs: Optimizing Performance:

Imagine adjusting the dials on a radio to find the perfect sound. Fine-tuning involves tweaking specific parameters within the LLM's internal structure. These adjustments influence how the LLM processes and generates text, optimizing its performance for your unique needs.

Code Example:

While the specific parameters you adjust would depend on the chosen LLM and your task, consider fine-tuning parameters related to:

- **Attention mechanism:** This helps the LLM focus on relevant parts of the input data when generating text, which can be crucial for writing accurate and context-specific comments.
- **Temperature:** This controls the "creativity" of the generated text. A lower temperature might lead to more predictable and safe comments, while a higher temperature could produce more creative but potentially risky outputs.

Remember, fine-tuning is a collaborative effort. You provide the data and guidance, and the LLM learns and adapts. The more you understand these core concepts and how they relate to code examples, the better equipped you'll be to unlock the true potential of fine-tuning for your coding projects.

In the next section, we'll explore the compelling reasons why you should consider fine-tuning LLMs and the benefits it can bring to your development workflow.

3.2. Why Fine-tune? Supercharge Your Projects with Personalized LLMs

Imagine having a coding assistant who not only understands your language but also speaks it fluently in the specific dialect of your project. That's the power of fine-tuning large language models (LLMs)! While pre-trained models are versatile, fine-tuning unlocks their true potential, tailoring them to your unique coding needs and boosting your development workflow. Let's explore the compelling reasons to consider this powerful technique, using concrete examples and code snippets for illustration:

1. Hyper-focused Solutions: Code Like a Jedi Master:

Think of it like using a Swiss Army knife versus a specialized surgical tool. A pre-trained LLM might get you decent results, but fine-tuning refines their abilities to a laser focus. Consider these scenarios:

Code generation:

- **Scenario:** You're working on a Python project involving complex mathematical calculations.
- **Pre-trained model:** You use a generic code generation model like GPT-J to write code for calculating the factorial of a number. It might generate basic code, but it might not be optimized for efficiency or clarity.
- **Fine-tuned model:** You fine-tune GPT-J on your project's codebase and relevant mathematical libraries. Now, you can provide a description like "Write a Python function to efficiently calculate the factorial of a large number using memoization," and the model generates code tailored to your project's specific requirements and coding style.

Code Example:

Pre-trained model:

Python

```python
def factorial(n):
  if n == 0:
    return 1
  else:
    return n * factorial(n-1)
```

Fine-tuned model:

Python

```python
from functools import cache


@cache
def optimized_factorial(n):
  if n == 0:
```

```
    return 1

  else:

    return n * optimized_factorial(n-1)
```

Translation:

- **Scenario:** You're working on a multilingual web application and need to translate code comments and documentation consistently.
- **Pre-trained model:** You use a general translation model like m2m_transformer to translate comments. While it might provide decent translations, it might miss technical nuances or project-specific terminology.
- **Fine-tuned model:** You fine-tune m2m_transformer on your codebase and existing translated comments. Now, it can translate comments while maintaining technical accuracy and consistency with your project's terminology.

Code Example:

Pre-trained model:

"Calculate the average value" translated to "Calcular el valor promedio" (generic translation)

Fine-tuned model:

"Calculate the average value using the pandas library" translated to "Calcular el valor promedio usando la biblioteca pandas" (maintains technical context)

2. Boosting Productivity: Unleash Your Inner Coding Machine:

Fine-tuning doesn't just enhance results; it streamlines your workflow. Imagine automating repetitive tasks and focusing on the bigger picture:

Repetitive code:

- **Scenario:** You need to write numerous unit tests for a new function.
- **Pre-trained model:** You write tests manually, which can be time-consuming and error-prone.
- **Fine-tuned model:** You fine-tune a model on existing test cases in your project. Now, you can provide the function's purpose and expected behavior, and the model generates basic test cases, freeing you to focus on complex edge cases.

Code Example:

Manual test:

Python

```python
def test_add_function():
```

```
assert add(2, 3) == 5
```

Fine-tuned model:

```
Python
```

```python
# Test case generated by the model:

def test_add_with_negative_numbers():

    assert add(-2, 3) == 1
```

Documentation writing:

- **Scenario:** You need to write comprehensive docstrings for a new library you're developing.
- **Pre-trained model:** Writing docstrings takes time away from actual development.
- **Fine-tuned model:** You fine-tune a model on existing docstrings in your project and documentation guidelines. Now, you can provide the function's purpose and parameters, and the model generates a draft docstring with basic structure and placeholders for additional information.

Code Example:

Manual docstring:

Python

```python
def my_function(param1, param2):

    """This function does something."""

    # ... function implementation ...
```

Fine-tuned model:

Python

```python
def my_function(param1: int, param2: str)
-> list:

    """This function takes two arguments and
```

3.3. Before You Fine-tune: Charting Your Course with Data, Resources, and Goals

Imagine setting sail on a coding adventure with your trusty LLM by your side. But before you raise the anchor, there are some crucial things to consider, like packing the right supplies and having a clear destination in mind. In the world of fine-tuning, these "supplies" are your data, resources, and goals. Let's explore each:

1. Data: The Fuel for Your Fine-tuning Engine:

Think of data as the food that keeps your LLM learning and growing. Here's what to keep in mind:

- **Relevance is key:** Your data should be highly relevant to your specific task and domain. Imagine fine-tuning a code generation model – feeding it general text won't do. You need code examples, documentation, and technical Q&A data related to your project.
- **Quality matters:** Clean, accurate, and well-formatted data leads to better fine-tuning results. Imagine training your LLM on code riddled with errors – it might learn those errors too!
- **Quantity is important:** More data generally leads to better fine-tuning, but quality always trumps quantity. A smaller dataset of high-quality, relevant data is often more valuable than a massive one that's irrelevant or noisy.

Code Example:

Suppose you're fine-tuning a model for **code translation** in your Python project. Here's what you'd need:

- **Relevant data:** Python code paired with corresponding translations in your target language. Ideally, code from your project or similar domains.
  - Example:

Python

```python
def calculate_area(length, width):

    return length * width
```

-

Python

```python
def calcular_area(largo, ancho):

    return largo * ancho
```

- **Quality:** Ensure the code is functional, error-free, and well-commented. The translations should be accurate and consistent.
- **Quantity:** While more data is generally better, aim for at least a few hundred high-quality code-translation pairs for a good starting point.

2. Resources: Making Sure You Have the Tools for the Job:

Fine-tuning can be computationally demanding, so consider these resources:

- **Hardware:** Depending on the model and dataset size, you might need a powerful GPU or access to cloud computing resources.
- **Software:** Ensure you have the necessary libraries and tools like Transformers and Hugging Face datasets installed and configured correctly.
- **Time:** Fine-tuning can take time, so factor that into your project timeline. Consider starting with smaller models and datasets if you're new to the process.

Code Example:

Let's say you're fine-tuning a large pre-trained model like Codex on your project's data. You'll likely need:

- **Hardware:** A GPU with sufficient memory is recommended, especially for larger datasets. Cloud platforms like Google Colab or Amazon SageMaker offer GPU access.
- **Software:** Install the Transformers library (pip install transformers) and ensure you have compatible versions of other required libraries.
- **Time:** Depending on the model size, dataset size, and hardware, fine-tuning could take hours or even days. Start with smaller datasets and models for quicker initial experiments.

3. Goals: Setting Your Fine-tuning Compass:

Having clear goals is crucial for a successful fine-tuning journey:

- **Specificity is key:** Define what you want to achieve with fine-tuning. Do you want to improve code generation accuracy, translate documentation more efficiently, or experiment with a new coding assistant?
- **Metrics matter:** Establish measurable metrics to track your progress. For example, if you're fine-tuning for code generation, track the accuracy and relevance of generated code compared to your baseline.
- **Realistic expectations:** Fine-tuning isn't magic. Set realistic and achievable goals based on your data, resources, and the capabilities of the chosen LLM.

Code Example:

Imagine your goal is to fine-tune a model for generating **unit tests** in your Python project. Here's how you can define your goals:

- **Specificity:** Improve the accuracy and coverage of automatically generated unit tests compared to manually written ones.
- **Metrics:** Track the percentage of tests that pass, their code coverage, and the time saved compared to manual testing.
- **Realistic expectations:** Aim for gradual improvement, as achieving human-level test writing accuracy might

not be feasible depending on the complexity of your codebase.

Remember, fine-tuning is a collaborative effort between you and the LLM. By carefully considering data, resources, and goals, you'll chart a course for success and unlock the true potential of this powerful technique in your coding endeavors.

In the next chapter, we'll delve deeper into the exciting world of selecting the right LLM for your specific needs. We'll equip you with the knowledge and tools to navigate the diverse LLM landscape and choose the perfect partner for your fine-tuning journey!

Get ready to match your project's unique requirements with the ideal LLM, setting the stage for remarkable coding achievements!

Congratulations On Reaching This Point!

You've successfully completed the first few chapters and are well on your way to unlocking the power of Fine-tuning Hugging Face. This journey has just begun, and exciting discoveries await you in the upcoming chapters.

As you continue learning, I would greatly appreciate your feedback on this book. ***Leaving a review on your preferred platform helps others discover this valuable resource and allows me to continue creating content that empowers learners like you.***

If you're interested in exploring other topics related to programming, data analysis, or technology, I encourage you to check out my other books. You can find a list of my books by searching for Chris C. Thompson

Happy learning, and keep exploring the fascinating world of Hugging Face!

Part 2: Mastering the Fine-tuning Process

CHAPTER 4

Selecting the Right Pre-trained Model - Your Coding BFF in the Making

So, you're ready to embark on the fine-tuning adventure with your trusty LLM by your side! But before you dive in, there's one crucial step: choosing the perfect pre-trained model. Think of it like picking the right teammate for your coding project. You wouldn't just grab any random person, right? You'd find someone with the skills and experience that match your specific needs.

In this chapter, we'll navigate the exciting (and sometimes overwhelming) world of pre-trained models on Hugging Face. We'll equip you with the knowledge to select the ideal model for your project, ensuring a smooth and successful fine-tuning journey.

4.1. Unveiling the Pre-trained Model Zoo: Finding Your Coding Partner on Hugging Face

Imagine a bustling marketplace filled with skilled professionals, each with unique talents. That's essentially the Hugging Face Hub, overflowing with pre-trained models ready to become your coding partner. But with so many options, choosing the right one can feel overwhelming. Fear not! This section equips you with the knowledge to navigate this exciting landscape and find the perfect model for your project.

Size Matters:

Just like picking the right tool for the job, consider your project's needs and resources when choosing a model size. Think of it like this:

- **Tiny models:** Think nimble and efficient, perfect for smaller tasks or resource-constrained environments. Examples: distilbert-base (66M parameters), t5-small (60M parameters).

Code Example:

Building a simple script that translates common error messages in your Python code? A tiny model like distilbert-base might suffice. You can load it with minimal hardware requirements and fine-tune it on your specific error message translations.

Python

```python
from transformers import
AutoModelForSequenceClassification,
AutoTokenizer


model_name = "distilbert-base-uncased"

tokenizer =
AutoTokenizer.from_pretrained(model_name)

model =
AutoModelForSequenceClassification.from_pr
etrained(model_name, num_labels=2)  # 2
for error/not error


# Sample training data (error message,
label)

train_data = [
    ("ModuleNotFoundError: No module named
'pandas'", 1),
    ("ValueError: could not convert string
to float: 'abc'", 1),
```

```python
        ("No    such    file   or   directory:
'myfile.txt'", 1),

        ("IndexError:    list    index    out    of
range", 1),

        ("Your    code    is    working perfectly!",
0),

    ]
```

```python
# ... Train the model on your data ...
```

- **Medium models:** More muscle for more complex tasks, balancing power and efficiency. Examples: bert-base-uncased (110M parameters), gpt2 (1.5B parameters).

Code Example:

Developing a more complex tool that generates Python code snippets based on natural language descriptions? A medium model like bert-base-uncased could handle it. It offers more capabilities than tiny models but still runs on most laptops.

Python

```python
from transformers import AutoModelForSeq2SeqLM, AutoTokenizer

model_name = "bert-base-uncased"

tokenizer = AutoTokenizer.from_pretrained(model_name)

model = AutoModelForSeq2SeqLM.from_pretrained(model_name)


# Sample training data (description, code snippet)
train_data = [
    ("Read data from CSV file and calculate average value", "df = pd.read_csv('data.csv'); average = df['column_name'].mean()"),

    ("Create a bar chart to visualize customer ages", "sns.barplot(x='age', y='count', data=df)")
]
```

```python
# ... Train the model on your data ...
```

- **Large models:** Heavyweight champions for demanding tasks, offering impressive capabilities but requiring more computational power. Examples: gpt-j-6b (6B parameters), t5-3b (3B parameters).

Code Example:

Tackling a massive project involving code translation across multiple languages? A large model like t5-3b might be the answer. However, be prepared for the need for powerful hardware (GPUs) and potentially longer training times.

Python

```python
from         transformers         import
AutoModelForSeq2SeqLM, AutoTokenizer


model_name = "t5-3b"

tokenizer                                    =
AutoTokenizer.from_pretrained(model_name)
```

```python
model                              =
AutoModelForSeq2SeqLM.from_pretrained(mode
l_name)


# Sample training data (source code,
translated code)
train_data = [

    ("def my_function(x): return x * 2",
"function my_function(x): return x * 2"),

    ("for i in range(5): print(i)", "for i
in range(5): print(i)")

]


# ... Train the model on your data, likely
using cloud resources for hardware ...
```

Remember: This is just a starting point! Explore the Hugging Face Hub using keywords and filters to discover models relevant to your project and experiment with different options. Consider the balance between model size, capabilities, and your hardware constraints.

Pro Tip: Start with a smaller model for initial experimentation and gradually scale up if needed. This helps you assess the feasibility of your project and fine-tuning approach before committing

4.2. Matchmaker, Matchmaker, Make Me a Model: Finding Your Perfect LLM Partner

Now that you've explored the diverse talent pool of pre-trained models on Hugging Face, it's time to find your ideal match! Think of it like casting the perfect role in a movie – you need someone who excels in the specific skills your project demands. This section will guide you through choosing the right LLM based on your project's unique needs.

Code Generation Matchmaking:

- **Task:** Generating code snippets or comments based on natural language descriptions.
- **Perfect Partners:**
    - Codex: Trained specifically on code, making it a natural language whiz in the coding world.
    - gpt-j-6b: A versatile powerhouse, but might require more fine-tuning for code generation tasks.

Code Example:

Imagine building a tool that generates Python code for data analysis tasks based on user descriptions. Codex might be your best bet:

```python
Python

from transformers import pipeline


code_gen = pipeline("text-to-code",
model="EleutherAI/code-gpt-jax-6b")

description = "Write a function to
calculate the average temperature from a
list of daily values."

generated_code = code_gen(description)

print(generated_code)    # Might output:
"def
calculate_average_temperature(temperatures
): ..."
```

Translation Matchmaking:

- **Task:** Translating code comments, documentation, or even entire codebases to different languages.
- **Perfect Partners:**

- o m2m_transformer: Specifically designed for machine translation, adept at handling code-specific nuances.
- o opus-mt-en-es: A multilingual powerhouse, pre-trained on translating various languages, including code-related content.

Code Example:

Developing a Python library with documentation that needs translation into Spanish. m2m_transformer could be your translator:

Python

```python
from transformers import pipeline


translator = pipeline("translation", model="Helsinki-NLP/opus-mt-en-es")

text = "This function reads data from a CSV file."

translated_text = translator(text)

print(translated_text[0]["translation"])
# Output: "Esta función lee datos de un archivo CSV."
```

Documentation Writing Matchmaking:

- **Task:** Generating initial drafts of documentation based on your code comments or API specifications.
- **Perfect Partners:**
  - bart-base: Skilled at summarizing information and generating coherent text, a great starting point for documentation.
  - t5-base: Flexible and adaptable, but might require more domain-specific fine-tuning for optimal documentation generation.

Code Example:

Building a new Python function for data visualization and need help with initial docstrings. bart-base can get you started:

Python

```python
from transformers import pipeline


doc_writer = pipeline("text-generation",
model="facebook/bart-base")

prompt = "Write a docstring for a function
named `create_bar_chart` that takes data
as input and generates a bar chart."

docstring                                    =
doc_writer(prompt)[0]["generated_text"]
```

```
print(docstring)          # Might output:
"""Creates a bar chart to visualize the
distribution of data."""
```

Remember: This is just a glimpse into the possibilities. Experiment with different models and explore the Hugging Face Hub for even more specialized options. Consider factors like your project's domain, the amount of data you have for fine-tuning, and your computational resources when making your final decision.

Pro Tip: Don't be afraid to get creative! Combine multiple models or leverage their strengths in different aspects of your project. The key is to find the LLM that best compliments your coding endeavors and unlocks your project's full potential.

4.3. Fine-tuning Feast: Catering to Different Model Appetites

Now that you've found your perfect pre-trained model match, it's time to prepare for the fine-tuning feast! Remember, different models have different preferences and needs, just like guests at a party. This section equips you with the know-how to cater to their specific "dietary" requirements for optimal results.

Transformer Treats:

- **Strengths:** Popular for various tasks, generally fine-tunable.
- **Considerations:**
  - **Resourceful:** Can be computationally expensive, especially larger models. Consider your hardware limitations.
  - **Hyperparameter picky:** Finding the right balance of hyperparameters during fine-tuning can be crucial for success. Experiment and track results.

Code Example:

Imagine you're fine-tuning gpt-j-6b for code generation (a hungry guest!). Be prepared to:

- **Serve up powerful hardware:** A GPU is recommended for efficient training. Think of it as providing a high-performance kitchen for complex recipe execution.
- **Adjust hyperparameters carefully:** Experiment with the "ingredients" like learning rate, batch size, and other parameters to optimize performance. It's like finding the perfect seasoning for your dish.

Python

```python
# Sample hyperparameter tuning loop

for learning_rate in [1e-4, 1e-5]:

    for batch_size in [8, 16]:
```

```
        # Train the model with different
hyperparameter combinations

        # Track and compare performance
metrics to find the optimal recipe
```

Autoregressive Appetizers:

- **Strengths:** Excel at generating text sequences like code or summaries.
- **Considerations:**
  - **Data hungry:** Often require more data for fine-tuning compared to other models. Prepare high-quality, relevant data specific to your task. Think of it as needing more diverse and specific ingredients for their specialized dishes.
  - **Fine-tuning finesse:** Careful attention to fine-tuning parameters and techniques is crucial for achieving desired results. It's like mastering the cooking technique to bring out the best flavor.

Code Example:

Fine-tuning gpt2 for Python comments (a delicate appetizer!) might require:

- **Large dataset of code with comments:** Ensure it covers your project's domain and style. Think of it as using fresh, local ingredients that match the dish's theme.

- **Custom loss function:** Consider using a loss function tailored to comment generation, like perplexity or BLEU score. It's like using a specialized sauce to enhance the overall experience.

Python

```python
# Define a custom loss function for comment generation

def custom_loss(predictions, labels):

    # Implement your loss function logic here, considering perplexity or BLEU score

    return loss_value


# Train the model using the custom loss function

model.compile(loss=custom_loss, optimizer='adam')

model.fit(X_train, y_train, ...)
```

Encoder-Decoder Delights:

- **Strengths:** Great for translation tasks with input and output languages.
- **Considerations:**
    - **Paired data preference:** Typically require paired data, like code-translation examples, for effective fine-tuning. Think of it as needing both the main course and its translated counterpart.
    - **Domain expertise:** Choose a model pre-trained on similar domains for better understanding of terminology and nuances. It's like using a chef familiar with the specific cuisine.

Code Example:

Fine-tuning m2m_transformer for code translation (a complex multi-course meal!) might require:

- **Dataset of code-translation pairs:** Ensure the code and translations are relevant to your project's domain and terminology. Think of it as having high-quality ingredients specifically suited for the dish.
- **Domain-specific pre-training:** Look for models pre-trained on code or software documentation for best results. It's like choosing a chef with experience in the desired style of cuisine.

Python

```
# Load a dataset of code-translation pairs
(code, translated_code)

train_data = ...



# Select a model pre-trained on code or
software documentation

model                              =
AutoModelForSeq2SeqLM.from_pretrained("Hel
sinki-NLP/opus-mt-en-es")



# Train   the   model   on   the   paired
code-translation dataset

model.compile(loss='categorical_crossentro
py', optimizer='adam')

model.fit(X_train, y_train, ...)
```

Remember: These are just general guidelines. Always refer to the specific model documentation and experiment to find the optimal fine-tuning approach for your chosen model and task.

In the next chapter, we'll delve into the exciting world of putting your chosen model to work! We'll explore the fine-tuning process, from data preparation to evaluation, equipping you with the practical steps to transform your pre-trained model into your personalized coding companion. Get ready to unleash the power of fine-tuning and watch your coding workflow soar!

CHAPTER 5

Data Preparation: The Fuel for Fine-tuning

Imagine your pre-trained LLM as a powerful engine, ready to supercharge your coding workflow. But just like any engine, it needs the right fuel to perform at its best. In this chapter, we'll delve into the crucial world of **data preparation**, the essential ingredient for successful fine-tuning.

5.1. Identifying and Collecting Data for Your Specific Task: Finding the Perfect Fuel Mix

Imagine your pre-trained LLM as a high-performance engine, ready to supercharge your coding workflow. But just like any engine, it needs the right fuel – data – to perform at its best. In this section, we'll explore how to identify and collect the perfect fuel mix for your specific fine-tuning task.

Think Like a Chef:

Remember, you wouldn't use the same ingredients for every dish, right? Similarly, the data you feed your LLM needs to be carefully chosen and tailored to your project's specific needs. Here's the recipe for success:

1. Define Your Task Clearly:

What exactly do you want your LLM to achieve? Generate code snippets, translate documentation, or write unit tests? Having a clear goal helps you identify the data that fuels it best.

Code Examples:

- **Task:** Generate Python code for data analysis based on user descriptions.
  - ○ **Data Sources:** GitHub repositories with Python data analysis projects, Kaggle datasets containing Python code for data manipulation, Stack Overflow Q&A related to Python data analysis code generation.
- **Task:** Translate Python docstrings into Spanish for better documentation accessibility.
  - ○ **Data Sources:** Open-source Python libraries with well-documented code and translated versions, datasets of code-comment pairs where comments are provided in both English and Spanish.
- **Task:** Write unit tests for newly written Python functions based on their functionality.
  - ○ **Data Sources:** Existing unit test suites for similar functions, code examples with corresponding test cases, datasets of function descriptions paired with unit test code.

2. Seek Quality Ingredients:

Remember, garbage in, garbage out! Ensure your data is:

*Relevant: Directly related to your project's domain and task. Don't feed your LLM irrelevant data; it won't magically become relevant!

* Clean: Free from typos, inconsistencies, and errors. Imagine throwing dirty vegetables into your engine – not a good recipe for success.

* Accurate: Contains reliable and truthful information. Feeding your LLM inaccurate data leads to inaccurate results.

Code Examples:

- **Cleaning Code-Related Data:**
  - Removing irrelevant comments or code blocks that don't contribute to your specific task (e.g., comments about project setup unrelated to code generation).
  - Standardizing variable names and coding styles for consistency (e.g., converting all variable names to lowercase with underscores).
  - Fixing typos and other errors in code and comments using tools like linters or manual inspection.

3. Explore Different Data Sources:

Don't limit yourself to just one source! Look for diverse data that captures different aspects of your task and domain. Think of it as using a variety of ingredients to enrich your dish.

- **Public repositories:** GitHub, GitLab, and other platforms offer code from various projects and domains.
- **Kaggle datasets:** Explore datasets specifically related to your task or containing code examples.
- **Stack Overflow Q&A:** Search for questions and answers relevant to your specific coding challenges.
- **Domain-specific forums and communities:** Look for online communities where developers discuss and share code in your domain.

4. Consider Pre-processed Datasets:

Save time and effort by using pre-processed datasets specifically designed for your task. These datasets often come clean, labeled, and ready-to-use for fine-tuning.

- **Hugging Face Hub:** Search for datasets tagged with your task or domain for pre-processed options.
- **Task-specific repositories:** Look for GitHub repositories maintained by researchers or organizations offering datasets for your specific fine-tuning task.

Remember: This is just the beginning! Experiment with different data sources, cleaning techniques, and pre-processed datasets to find the perfect fuel mix for your project's specific needs. By providing your LLM with high-quality and relevant data, you'll set it up for success in the next stage: preprocessing!

Pro Tip: Start small! Begin with a smaller dataset to test your fine-tuning approach and data preparation techniques. Once you're confident, you can scale up to larger datasets for even better results.

5.2. Data Cleaning and Preprocessing Techniques: Refining Your Fuel for Peak Performance

Imagine you've gathered a basket of ingredients for your LLM's fine-tuning feast. But before you toss them in the pot, some prep work is crucial! In this section, we'll explore essential data cleaning and preprocessing techniques to refine your fuel for optimal model performance.

Think of it like this: Raw ingredients rarely go straight into a dish. You peel, chop, and season them to enhance their flavor and make them easier to use. Similarly, data preprocessing transforms your raw data into a format your LLM can understand and effectively learn from.

1. Cleaning Up the Mess:

- **Remove impurities:** Eliminate irrelevant information like comments, extra lines, or unnecessary characters. Imagine taking out wilted leaves or dirt from your vegetables.
- **Standardize formatting:** Ensure consistent formatting across your data, like using the same units or

capitalization styles. Think of using the same chopping style for all your ingredients.

- **Fix errors:** Identify and correct typos, inconsistencies, or missing values. It's like checking for rotten spots and removing them before cooking.

Code Example:

Cleaning code-related data might involve:

Python

```python
# Remove comments that don't contribute to
code generation

import re


def clean_code(text):

  return re.sub(r"#.*?\n", "", text)


# Standardize variable names

def standardize_names(text):

  return text.lower().replace("-", "_")
```

```
# Fix typos using libraries like `nltk` or
manual inspection
```

2. Breaking Down the Ingredients:

- **Tokenization:** Break down text data into smaller units (tokens) like words or characters. Imagine chopping your vegetables into bite-sized pieces.
- **Numerical encoding:** Convert categorical data (e.g., colors, labels) into numerical representations for the LLM to understand. Think of assigning numbers to different spices based on their heat level.

Code Example:

Tokenizing code might involve:

```
Python
```

```python
from transformers import AutoTokenizer


tokenizer                                =
AutoTokenizer.from_pretrained("gpt2")

code_text = "def my_function(x): return x
* 2"

tokens = tokenizer.tokenize(code_text)
```

```
print(tokens)          #     Output:     ['def',
'my_function',    '(',      'x',      ')',      ':',
'return', 'x', '*', '2']
```

3. Balancing the Flavors:

- **Oversampling/undersampling:** Address imbalanced datasets where certain categories have much less data. Imagine adding more of a rare spice to balance the flavor profile.
- **Data augmentation:** Artificially create new data points to increase dataset size and diversity. Think of using different cooking techniques to create variations of the same dish.

Code Example:

Oversampling a minority class in code comments:

```Python
from imblearn.over_sampling import SMOTE


smote = SMOTE(random_state=42)
```

```
X_resampled,          y_resampled          =
smote.fit_resample(X_train_minority,
y_train_minority)
```

Remember: Data cleaning and preprocessing are iterative processes. Experiment with different techniques and evaluate their impact on your LLM's performance. The goal is to provide clean, well-structured, and informative data that fuels your fine-tuning journey towards success!

Pro Tip: Leverage libraries like pandas for data cleaning, transformers for tokenization, and imblearn for balancing techniques. These libraries offer efficient tools to streamline your data preparation process.

In the next section, we'll explore how to structure your refined data for optimal model training, ensuring your LLM gets the most out of its delicious fuel!

5.3. Structuring Your Data for Optimal Model Training: Serving the Fuel the Right Way

Imagine you've meticulously prepped your ingredients, cleaned them, chopped them, and even added some secret spices! But before tossing them into the pot, how you arrange them matters. In this section, we'll explore structuring your data for optimal model training, ensuring your LLM gets the most out of its fine-tuning feast.

Think of it like this: Imagine presenting a well-plated dish. You wouldn't just dump everything on the plate in a pile, right? Similarly, structuring your data involves organizing it into formats that your LLM can efficiently consume and learn from.

1. Dividing Up the Portions:

- **Train-validation-test split:** Separate your data into distinct sets:
  - **Training set:** The largest portion (usually 80%) used to train your LLM. Think of it as the main ingredient for your dish.
  - **Validation set:** A smaller portion (usually 10%) used to monitor model performance during training and adjust hyperparameters. It's like tasting your dish while cooking to check seasoning.
  - **Test set:** The smallest portion (usually 10%) used for final evaluation after training is complete. It's like presenting the finished dish to a guest for their unbiased feedback.

Code Example:

Python

```
from    sklearn.model_selection    import
train_test_split
```

```python
X_train, X_val, X_test, y_train, y_val,
y_test     =     train_test_split(X,    y,
test_size=0.2, random_state=42)
```

2. Batching for Efficient Cooking:

- **Dataloaders:** Use libraries like Dataloaders or Datasets to load and batch your data efficiently during training. Imagine portioning your ingredients into manageable batches for cooking instead of throwing everything in at once.
- **Padding:** Adjust data lengths within each batch to match your model's requirements. Think of making sure all your ingredients fit the size and proportions of your dish.

Code Example:

Python

```python
from        transformers        import
DataCollatorForLanguageModeling


tokenizer                              =
AutoTokenizer.from_pretrained("gpt2")
```

```python
dataloader                              =
DataCollatorForLanguageModeling(tokenizer=
tokenizer, mlm=True)


batch  =  dataloader([tokenizer(text)  for
text in X_train[:8]])

print(batch["input_ids"].shape)  # Output:
torch.Size([8,  64])  (batch  size,  max
sequence length)
```

3. Monitoring the Flavor:

- **Define metrics:** Track relevant metrics during training to evaluate your LLM's performance. Imagine using a thermometer to ensure your dish cooks at the right temperature.
- **Early stopping:** Stop training if performance plateaus or starts to decline, preventing overfitting. It's like knowing when to take your dish off the heat before it burns.

Code Example:

Python

```python
from transformers import TrainingArguments

training_args = TrainingArguments(

    output_dir="./results",

    num_train_epochs=3,

    per_device_train_batch_size=8,

    evaluation_strategy="epoch",

    metric_for_best_model="accuracy",

)
```

Remember: Structuring your data is an ongoing process. Experiment with different splitting strategies, batch sizes, and metrics to find the optimal configuration for your specific task and model. The goal is to present your LLM with well-organized and informative data, paving the way for a successful fine-tuning journey!

Pro Tip: Consider using preprocessing pipelines from libraries like transformers or datasets. These pipelines offer convenient ways to perform common data preparation steps in a structured and efficient manner.

In the next chapter, we'll finally dive into the exciting world of putting your prepared data to work! We'll explore the fine-tuning process step-by-step, from model configuration to evaluation, empowering you to unleash the full potential of your LLM-powered coding companion. So, get ready to turn up the heat and cook up some amazing results!

CHAPTER 6

Fine-tuning in Action: A Step-by-Step Guide

Ready to unlock the true potential of your pre-trained LLM? Buckle up, because Chapter 6 takes you on a hands-on journey through the world of fine-tuning! We'll explore the tools, configurations, and steps to transform your LLM from a general-purpose language model into a coding companion tailor-made for your specific tasks.

6.1. Choosing Your Development Framework: The Kitchen Tools You Need

Imagine you're about to whip up a culinary masterpiece. You wouldn't just grab any old pot and pan, right? You'd choose the right tools based on the recipe, your skill level, and what you have in your kitchen. The same goes for fine-tuning your LLM – you need the right **development framework**. Think of it as your coding kitchen, equipped with specific tools to help you achieve your culinary (or in this case, coding) goals!

Here are some popular frameworks to consider, each with its own strengths and quirks:

PyTorch:

- **Pros:** Beginner-friendly, flexible, large community for support. Imagine it as a well-equipped kitchen with intuitive appliances, perfect for learning the ropes. You can easily find online tutorials and forums to troubleshoot any issues.

Code Example (PyTorch):

Python

```python
from                  transformers              import
AutoModelForSequenceClassification,
AutoTokenizer, Trainer



# Replace with your chosen model and task

model_name = "bert-base-uncased"

num_labels = 2   # Adjust based on your
classification task



# Load pre-trained model and tokenizer

model                                          =
AutoModelForSequenceClassification.from_pr
```

```python
etrained(model_name,
num_labels=num_labels)

tokenizer                          =
AutoTokenizer.from_pretrained(model_name)


# ... (rest of the code for loading data,
defining    training    configuration,    and
training the model)
```

- **Cons:** Might require more manual coding compared to other options. Think of it like needing to understand all the knobs and dials on your appliances.

TensorFlow:

- **Pros:** Powerful, scalable, well-suited for complex tasks. Imagine it as a professional kitchen with industrial-grade tools for serious cooking. It can handle large datasets and demanding computations efficiently.

Code Example (TensorFlow):

Python

```python
from tensorflow import keras

from transformers import TFBertModel
```

```python
# Load pre-trained model

bert_model                                    =
TFBertModel.from_pretrained("bert-base-unc
ased")


# Build your fine-tuning model
architecture

input_ids = keras.Input(shape=(max_len,),
dtype=tf.int32)

outputs = bert_model(input_ids)

# ... (add layers for your specific task,
like classification or generation)

model     =     keras.Model(inputs=input_ids,
outputs=output_layer)


# ... (rest of the code for training the
model)
```

- **Cons:** Steeper learning curve compared to PyTorch. Think of it like needing to understand complex cooking techniques and equipment configurations.

Hugging Face Transformers:

- **Pros:** Pre-built libraries and pipelines specifically designed for working with LLMs. Imagine it as a kitchen specifically stocked for working with advanced ingredients like pre-trained models. Easy to get started with fine-tuning, with lots of ready-made components.

Code Example (Hugging Face Transformers):

Python

```python
from transformers import AutoModelForSequenceClassification, AutoTokenizer, Trainer


# Define your fine-tuning task and model

task_name = "text-classification"

model_name = "bert-base-uncased"


# Load model and tokenizer
```

```python
model = AutoModelForSequenceClassification.from_pretrained(model_name, num_labels=2)

tokenizer = AutoTokenizer.from_pretrained(model_name)


# Load your data
train_dataset = load_dataset("text", split="train")


# Define training configuration
training_args = TrainingArguments(output_dir="./results", num_train_epochs=3)


# Create a Trainer object with pre-built pipeline
trainer = Trainer(
    model=model,
```

```
    args=training_args,

    train_dataset=train_dataset,

    compute_metrics=task_name,

)


# Train the model!

trainer.train()
```

- **Cons:** Might be less flexible for highly customized workflows. Think of it like having some pre-made meals you can heat up, but limited options for creating your own dishes from scratch.

Choosing the Right Tool:

Ultimately, the best framework depends on your:

- **Comfort level:** Are you a coding beginner or a seasoned expert?
- **Project needs:** Do you have a simple task or a complex one requiring high performance?
- **Personal preferences:** Do you prefer more flexibility or pre-built components?

Explore & Experiment:

Don't be afraid to try out different frameworks! Many offer tutorials and documentation to help you get started. The key is to find the one that feels most comfortable and efficient for you. Remember, the perfect framework is the one that helps you cook up amazing results with your LLM!

6.2. Building the Fine-tuning Pipeline: Your Recipe for Success

Congratulations on choosing your development framework! Now, it's time to get your hands dirty and build the actual fine-tuning pipeline. Think of it like preparing a delicious recipe – you gather your ingredients, follow the steps, and adjust as needed to create a masterpiece. In this case, your masterpiece is a fine-tuned LLM ready to tackle your coding tasks!

Ingredients:

1. **Pre-trained Model:** This is your base ingredient, like flour or eggs in a cake. Choose a model suited to your task (e.g., code generation, translation).
2. **Data:** This is the fuel for your LLM's learning, like the spices and flavors in your recipe. Ensure it's clean, relevant, and well-structured (see Chapter 5 for tips).
3. **Tokenizer:** This breaks down your data into understandable pieces for the LLM, like chopping vegetables for your dish. Choose a tokenizer compatible with your model.

Code Example (PyTorch):

Python

```python
from transformers import
AutoModelForSequenceClassification,
AutoTokenizer


# Replace with your chosen model and task

model_name = "bert-base-uncased"

num_labels = 2  # Adjust based on your
classification task


# Load pre-trained model and tokenizer

model =
AutoModelForSequenceClassification.from_pr
etrained(model_name,
num_labels=num_labels)

tokenizer =
AutoTokenizer.from_pretrained(model_name)
```

The Recipe:

1. **Define the Task:** Clearly specify what you want your LLM to achieve (e.g., generate code, translate text). This guides the training process.
2. **Configure the Training:** Set parameters like learning rate, number of training epochs, and loss function. Think of it as adjusting oven temperature and cooking time.

Code Example (TensorFlow):

Python

```
from tensorflow import keras
```

```
# Define loss function and optimizer
loss_fn                                    =
keras.losses.SparseCategoricalCrossentropy
(from_logits=True)

optimizer                                  =
keras.optimizers.Adam(learning_rate=2e-5)
```

3. **Build the Training Loop:** This is where the magic happens! The LLM learns from your data, iteratively improving its performance based on your recipe.

Imagine following the steps in your recipe and checking on your dish in the oven.

Code Example (Hugging Face Transformers):

Python

```python
from transformers import Trainer


# Create a Trainer object with your configuration

training_args = TrainingArguments(output_dir="./results", num_train_epochs=3)

trainer = Trainer(

    model=model,

    args=training_args,

    train_dataset=your_train_dataset,

)


# Train the model!

trainer.train()
```

Pro Tip: Leverage pre-built pipelines from libraries like Hugging Face Transformers. They streamline common steps and offer convenient ways to experiment with different configurations.

Remember: Fine-tuning is an iterative process. Experiment with different settings, monitor your LLM's performance with metrics like accuracy or loss, and don't be afraid to adjust your recipe as needed. The goal is to create a perfectly trained LLM that becomes your go-to coding companion!

In the next step: We'll explore how to put your fine-tuned LLM to work, showcasing practical applications and exciting examples to unleash its full potential! So, stay tuned and get ready to code like never before!

6.3. Executing the Fine-tuning Process and Monitoring Progress: Watching Your Dish Come to Life!

With your recipe (fine-tuning configuration) in hand and ingredients (pre-trained model, data, tokenizer) prepped, it's time to fire up the oven and start training! But don't just set it and forget it. Think of this phase like diligently checking on your dish as it cooks, making adjustments, and savoring the aroma of progress. Here's how to monitor your LLM's journey to coding mastery:

Monitoring Metrics:

- **Accuracy, Loss, and BLEU Score:** These are like thermometers telling you how well your LLM is learning based on your chosen task. Track them throughout training to identify trends and potential issues.
- **Visualization Tools:** Use tools like TensorBoard to plot graphs and visualize how metrics change over time. This helps you spot plateaus or sudden drops in performance, indicating areas for improvement.

Code Example (TensorBoard with TensorFlow):

Python

```python
from tensorflow.keras.callbacks import TensorBoard


tensorboard_callback = TensorBoard(log_dir="./logs")


# ... (train your model with tensorboard_callback as an argument)
```

Fine-tuning Hyperparameters:

Think of hyperparameters like the knobs and dials on your oven – adjusting them can optimize your LLM's performance. Experiment with:

- **Learning Rate:** Controls how quickly the LLM learns. Too high can lead to instability, too low can be slow.
- **Number of Epochs:** How many times the LLM sees all your data. More epochs can improve accuracy, but too many can lead to overfitting.

Code Example (Adjusting Learning Rate in PyTorch):

Python

```python
from transformers import AdamW


optimizer = AdamW(model.parameters(), lr=2e-5)  # Initial learning rate


# ... (after some training)


if loss > previous_loss:  # If loss starts increasing
    optimizer.lr *= 0.9   # Reduce learning rate slightly
```

previous_loss = loss

Early Stopping:

Don't let your LLM overcook! If performance plateaus or starts declining, consider stopping training early to prevent overfitting. This is like taking your dish out of the oven when it's perfectly done.

Code Example (Early Stopping with Hugging Face Transformers):

Python

```python
from transformers import TrainingArguments


training_args = TrainingArguments(
    output_dir="./results",
    num_train_epochs=3,
    early_stopping_patience=2   # Stop after 2 epochs without improvement
)
```

```
#    ...    (train    your    model    with
training_args)
```

Remember: Fine-tuning is an iterative process. Be patient, experiment, and don't get discouraged if you don't see perfect results immediately. With careful monitoring and adjustments, you'll gradually fine-tune your LLM into a powerful coding companion!

Pro Tip: Explore pre-built fine-tuning notebooks and tutorials from platforms like Hugging Face and Google AI. These resources provide step-by-step guidance and examples to help you get started quickly and efficiently.

In the next chapter: We'll showcase exciting ways to put your fine-tuned LLM to work on real-world coding tasks. Get ready to see how your LLM can help you code faster, smarter, and more creatively!

CHAPTER 7

Advanced Techniques for Fine-tuning Mastery

Congratulations! You've successfully navigated the basics of fine-tuning your LLM, transforming it from a pre-trained powerhouse into a coding companion tailor-made for your needs. But the journey doesn't stop there! Buckle up, because Chapter 7 dives into the world of advanced techniques, pushing the boundaries of your LLM's potential and unlocking even more exciting possibilities.

7.1. Hyperparameter Tuning: Optimizing for Peak Performance

Imagine you've crafted the perfect recipe for your LLM's fine-tuning journey, but even the most delicious dish can benefit from a sprinkle of extra seasoning, right? That's where **hyperparameter tuning** comes in – it's adjusting the knobs and dials of your fine-tuning process to squeeze out every ounce of potential from your LLM.

Think of it like fine-tuning the temperature and cooking time in your oven. While you have your recipe (configuration), experimenting with different **learning rates, batch sizes, and epochs** can significantly impact your LLM's performance. But don't worry, you're not stuck manually testing every combination! Powerful tools like **Bayesian optimization** and **grid search** help you explore the hyperparameter space efficiently, suggesting the most promising configurations to try.

Ready to become a hyperparameter chef? Here's a taste of what's cooking:

Ingredients:

- **Learning Rate:** Controls how quickly your LLM learns – too high can cause instability, too low is slow. Imagine adjusting the heat under your pan. A high learning rate might cook your dish too quickly, leaving it unevenly done, while a low rate might leave it raw.
- **Batch Size:** The number of data points processed at once. Larger batches can be faster, but smaller ones can be more stable for complex tasks. Think of how many ingredients you add to your pan at once. Throwing in everything at once might overwhelm the pan, while adding them gradually ensures even cooking.
- **Epochs:** How many times the LLM sees all your data. More epochs can improve accuracy, but too many can lead to overfitting (memorizing instead of learning). Like baking your dish for too long, it might look good initially but ultimately lack flavor and adaptability.

Tools & Resources:

- **Hugging Face Optuna integration:** https://huggingface.co/docs/transformers/en/main_classes/optimizer_schedules This tool uses Bayesian optimization to efficiently suggest promising hyperparameter combinations for you to try.
- **Ray Tune for hyperparameter tuning:** https://docs.ray.io/en/latest/tune/index.html Ray Tune offers various hyperparameter tuning algorithms, including grid search, random search, and Bayesian optimization, giving you flexibility in your approach.
- **A beginner's guide to hyperparameter tuning:** https://www.analyticsvidhya.com/blog/2022/02/a-comprehensive-guide-on-hyperparameter-tuning-and-its-techniques/ This guide provides a clear and concise introduction to hyperparameter tuning concepts and techniques.

Remember: Hyperparameter tuning is an ongoing process. Monitor your LLM's performance (accuracy, loss) and don't be afraid to adjust the dials as you go. With a bit of tweaking, you can unlock the peak performance hidden within your fine-tuned model!

Code Example (PyTorch, adjusting learning rate):

Python

```python
from transformers import AdamW
```

```
optimizer   =   AdamW(model.parameters(),
lr=2e-5)  # Initial learning rate


# ... (after some training)


if loss > previous_loss:  # If loss starts
increasing

   optimizer.lr *= 0.9  # Reduce learning
rate slightly


previous_loss = loss
```

Let's get hands-on with a real example! Imagine you're fine-tuning a sentiment analysis model to classify movie reviews as positive, negative, or neutral. Here's how you can apply hyperparameter tuning:

1. **Start with a baseline configuration:** Choose a common learning rate (e.g., 2e-5), batch size (e.g., 32), and number of epochs (e.g., 3). Train your model with this configuration and record the accuracy (e.g., 75%).
2. **Tune the learning rate:** Use Optuna or Ray Tune to explore different learning rates (e.g., 1e-5, 5e-5) while

keeping other parameters fixed. See which learning rate results in the highest accuracy. Let's say 3e-5 gives you 78% accuracy.

3. **Experiment with batch size:** Now, try different batch sizes (e.g., 16, 64) with the best learning rate (3e-5).

7.2. Multi-task Learning: Unleashing Your LLM's Inner Multitasker

Imagine your LLM is like a talented apprentice. Instead of mastering just one skill, wouldn't it be amazing to train it in coding, translating languages, and even writing poetry all at once? That's the power of **multi-task learning**, where you train your LLM on multiple related tasks simultaneously. Think of it like baking a multi-layered cake – each layer represents a different task, but the bottom layers (fundamental language understanding) are shared, saving you time and effort.

Why is this cool?

- **Efficiency Boost:** By sharing knowledge across tasks, your LLM learns faster and needs less data for each individual task. Imagine learning math and physics together – some concepts overlap, making you understand both better.

- **Performance Jump:** The shared knowledge strengthens your LLM's overall understanding, leading to better results on each individual task. Just like practicing different sports improves your overall fitness and coordination.

- **Versatility Unlocked:** A multi-task LLM becomes a multi-tool, ready to tackle various coding, language, and creative tasks. It's like having a Swiss Army knife for all your coding and language needs!

Ready to unleash your LLM's hidden talents? Here are some exciting applications:

- **Code with Explanations:** Train your LLM to not only write code but also explain its reasoning in plain English, making your code clear and maintainable. Imagine your LLM saying, "I used this function because..."
- **Translate & Summarize:** Translate text while simultaneously creating concise summaries, saving you time and resources. Get the gist of a foreign article while having its translation readily available.
- **Question & Answer Master:** Train your LLM to answer your questions and find relevant information from different sources, becoming your own personal research assistant. Ask your LLM "What are the best machine learning frameworks for image classification?" and get a comprehensive answer with supporting evidence.

Before you jump in:

- **Choose related tasks:** Tasks should share some skills or knowledge for efficient learning. Baking a cake and building a rocket might not be the best combo!

- **Prepare enough data:** Each task needs sufficient data for the LLM to learn effectively. Don't expect miracles with limited information.

Ready to explore? Here are some resources to get you started:

- **A gentle introduction to multi-task learning:** https://www.youtube.com/watch?v=5OZBgL1bxJA
- **Multi-task learning with transformers:** https://towardsdatascience.com/how-to-create-and-train-a-multi-task-transformer-model-18c54a146240
- **Examples of multi-task learning in NLP:** https://arxiv.org/pdf/1905.13540

Remember, multi-task learning can be more complex than single-task fine-tuning. But with careful planning and the right tools, you can unlock a whole new level of versatility from your LLM, transforming it into a true coding and language superpower!

Code Example (Hugging Face Transformers, multi-task classification):

Python

```
from transformers import
AutoModelForSequenceClassification,
AutoTokenizer
```

```python
# Define separate labels for each task

task1_labels = ["category1", "category2"]

task2_labels = ["labelA", "labelB"]


# Load pre-trained model and tokenizer

model_name = "bert-base-uncased"

model                                    =
AutoModelForSequenceClassification.from_pr
etrained(model_name,
num_labels=len(task1_labels)             +
len(task2_labels))

tokenizer                                =
AutoTokenizer.from_pretrained(model_name)


# Prepare your data:


# Combine data from both tasks, ensuring
each example has labels for both tasks
```

```
# ... (prepare data with labels for both
tasks)


# Train the model on both tasks
simultaneously

trainer = Trainer(

    model=model,


args=TrainingArguments(output_dir="./resul
ts"),

    train_dataset=your_combined_dataset,

)



trainer.train()
```

Stay tuned for the next chapter, where we dive into the world of transfer learning – leveraging pre-trained models to accelerate your LLM's learning journey!

7.3. Transfer Learning: Turbocharge Your LLM with Pre-trained Power

Imagine training your LLM for hours, only to realize it needs even more time to learn effectively. Enter **transfer learning**, the secret weapon that lets you **leverage pre-trained models** and **jumpstart your LLM's learning**. Think of it like building a house – instead of making every brick yourself, you use pre-made ones for the foundation, saving time and effort to focus on the unique features of your house.

Transfer learning offers several benefits:

- **Faster Training:** Pre-trained models already understand language fundamentals, so your LLM learns specific tasks much quicker. Imagine starting with a half-built house – you finish it faster than building from scratch.
- **Better Performance:** Pre-trained models are trained on massive datasets, giving your LLM a solid foundation for better task performance. It's like using high-quality materials for your house, leading to a sturdier and more beautiful final product.
- **Less Data Needed:** With pre-trained knowledge, your LLM needs less data to learn new tasks, saving you time and resources. It's like needing fewer bricks because you have a strong foundation.

Ready to unlock the power of pre-trained models? Here are some exciting applications:

- **Fine-tune for Text Generation:** Use a pre-trained model like GPT-3 to write different creative text formats (poems, scripts, code) instead of training from scratch. It's like using prefabricated elements to add unique features to your house, like a bay window or a rooftop terrace.
- **Translate Languages Efficiently:** Leverage pre-trained translation models like T5 to translate text between languages with high accuracy, even with limited data for your specific language pair. It's like using pre-made beams and trusses for your house, ensuring a strong and structurally sound translation "building."
- **Answer Your Questions Instantly:** Train a pre-trained model like Bard to answer your questions and summarize information from various sources, becoming your own personal AI assistant. It's like having pre-installed smart home features in your house, providing information and assistance readily.

But remember, it's not magic!

- **Choose the right model:** Select a pre-trained model relevant to your task and data. Building a beach house with mountain lodge materials wouldn't make sense!
- **Fine-tune effectively:** Don't just copy the pre-trained model – adapt it to your specific task for optimal results. Fine-tuning is like customizing your pre-fab elements to fit your house design perfectly.

Ready to explore? Here are some resources to get you started:

- **A beginner's guide to transfer learning:** https://www.analyticsvidhya.com/blog/2022/02/a-comprehensive-guide-on-hyperparameter-tuning-and-its-techniques/
- **Hugging Face Transformers library:** https://huggingface.co/transformers/
- **Fine-tuning a T5 model for translation:** [[invalid URL removed]]([invalid URL removed])

Remember, transfer learning can be a game-changer for your LLM projects. With the right approach and tools, you can unlock its full potential and build amazing things, faster and more efficiently!

Code Example (Hugging Face Transformers, fine-tuning T5 for sentiment analysis):

Python

```python
from transformers import T5Tokenizer, T5ForConditionalGeneration


# Load pre-trained T5 model and tokenizer
model_name = "t5-base"
tokenizer = T5Tokenizer.from_pretrained(model_name)
```

```python
model = T5ForConditionalGeneration.from_pretrained(model_name)


# Prepare your data for sentiment analysis (text and labels)


# Fine-tune the model on your data
trainer = Trainer(
    model=model,

    args=TrainingArguments(output_dir="./results"),

    train_dataset=your_sentiment_analysis_dataset,
)


trainer.train()
```

Stay tuned for the next chapter, where we explore advanced techniques like distillation and multimodal learning to push your LLM's capabilities even further!

Congratulations On Reaching This Point!

You've successfully completed the first few chapters and are well on your way to unlocking the power of Fine-tuning Hugging Face. This journey has just begun, and exciting discoveries await you in the upcoming chapters.

As you continue learning, I would greatly appreciate your feedback on this book. ***Leaving a review on your preferred platform helps others discover this valuable resource and allows me to continue creating content that empowers learners like you.***

If you're interested in exploring other topics related to programming, data analysis, or technology, I encourage you to check out my other books. You can find a list of my books by searching for Chris C. Thompson

Happy learning, and keep exploring the fascinating world of Hugging Face!

Part 3: Building Smarter Software with Fine-tuned LLMs

CHAPTER 8

Unleashing the Power in Your Projects

Hold onto your coding hats, because we're about to dive into the real world and see how LLMs can transform your projects from good to **mind-blowing**. Forget tedious tasks, frustrating searches, and information overload. With LLMs by your side, you'll be coding smarter, faster, and more creatively than ever before. Buckle up!

8.1. Code Generation: From Brainstorm to Built in a Blink

Imagine this: you're buzzing with an idea for a revolutionary fitness app that tracks activity and personalized workout routines. But the thought of writing countless lines of code for data management, user interface, and complex algorithms makes you want to hit the gym instead. Fear not, code warrior! LLMs (Large Language Models) are here to be your coding sidekick, generating code snippets, function outlines, and even entire scripts based on your ideas – **in a flash**.

Think of it as having a supercharged code completion tool on steroids. Describe your concept in plain English, and the LLM will whip up lines of code, saving you precious time and effort. But that's not all! LLMs can also:

- **Automate repetitive tasks:** Need to generate hundreds of lines of boilerplate code, like data structures or UI elements for your fitness app's exercise library? No sweat! The LLM handles it while you focus on the unique features that track heart rate, calculate calorie burn, and personalize workout intensity.
- **Test different code variations:** Trying out different algorithms for optimizing workout recommendations? LLMs can quickly generate code for various approaches, letting you compare and choose the most effective one for your fitness app users.
- **Boost your productivity:** Forget spending hours writing basic code for user logins, data storage, and progress tracking. Get the foundation laid down by the LLM, then focus on the innovative features that make your fitness app stand out, like gamification elements or social sharing capabilities.

Here are some real-world examples:

- **Web development:** Describe the functionality you want for your fitness app's user interface (e.g., exercise selection, progress charts, social media integration), and the LLM generates the HTML and CSS code to get you started.

- **Mobile app development:** Sketch out the core functionalities of your app (e.g., GPS tracking, workout logging, personalized recommendations), and the LLM writes basic code for data capture, sensor integration, and user interaction in languages like Swift or Kotlin.
- **Data analysis:** Explain what you want to analyze from user data (e.g., workout frequency, calorie burn trends, exercise preferences), and the LLM generates Python code to automate calculations, create visualizations, and identify user behavior patterns.

Ready to try it out? Here's some code to get you started (using Hugging Face Transformers):

Python

```python
from transformers import AutoTokenizer, AutoModelForSeq2SeqLM


# Load a pre-trained code generation model (e.g., Codex)

model_name = "facebook/code-davinci-003"

tokenizer = AutoTokenizer.from_pretrained(model_name)
```

```python
model = AutoModelForSeq2SeqLM.from_pretrained(mode
l_name)


# Describe your code idea in plain English

prompt = "Generate Python code for a
function that calculates the burned
calories based on exercise type, duration,
and user weight."


# Encode the prompt and user code context
(if any)

input_ids = tokenizer.encode(prompt,
return_tensors="pt")


# Generate code using the LLM

output = model.generate(

    input_ids,

    max_length=256,
```

```
    num_beams=4,

    early_stopping=True,

)


# Decode the generated code

generated_code                           =
tokenizer.decode(output[0],
skip_special_tokens=True)


# Print the generated code

print(generated_code)
```

Remember, this is just the beginning. As LLMs evolve, their code-generation capabilities will become even more sophisticated and nuanced. So, unleash your creativity, team up with your LLM, and start building the next generation of amazing applications!

P.S. Stay tuned for the next chapter, where we'll explore how LLMs can help you navigate your codebase like a pro with lightning-fast search and clear documentation generation!

8.2. Code Search and Navigation: Escape the Code Labyrinth

Imagine toiling away in a sprawling codebase, searching for a specific function like Indiana Jones hunting the Ark. Hours melt away, frustration mounts, and you're still lost in the digital jungle. Fear not, intrepid developer! LLMs (Large Language Models) are here to be your machete, hacking through the code wilderness with **intuitive searches and contextual understanding**.

Think of it like having Google for code, but way smarter. Instead of cryptic keywords, describe your quarry in plain English. Need to find all instances of a variable named "currentUser"? Just ask! Want to understand how a function interacts with others? Describe its behavior, and the LLM will map its connections within the codebase.

But LLMs are more than just search engines. They're code whisperers, understanding the language and relationships within your project:

- **Navigate by context:** Forget hopping between files blindly. LLMs grasp code structure, allowing you to say things like "show me functions related to login functionality" and be whisked to the relevant sections.
- **Explain the cryptic:** Unfamiliar code can be intimidating. LLMs analyze it, providing explanations in simple terms, demystifying its purpose and logic.
- **Boost code comprehension:** Quickly grasp the overall architecture by asking the LLM to summarize key

components and their interactions. Think of it as a code CliffsNotes!

Here are some real-world examples:

- **Open-source project:** Buried in a massive library? Ask the LLM to find all functions implementing a specific algorithm, like sorting or encryption.
- **Legacy codebase:** Deciphering undocumented code? Describe its behavior (e.g., "updates user data on form submission"), and the LLM might unlock its hidden logic.
- **Team collaboration:** Share your code and use the LLM to guide teammates to relevant sections or explain functionalities, fostering smoother communication and knowledge sharing.

Ready to wield this power? Here's some code to get you started (using Github Copilot):

Python   .

```python
# Install and activate Github Copilot in
your IDE

# ...



# Open your code file and position your
cursor where you want to search
```

```
# ...


# Type your search query in natural
language:

print("Copilot, find all functions that
modify the 'cart' object.")


# Copilot will highlight relevant code
snippets and even suggest potential
completions based on your query and code
context.
```

Remember, this is just a taste of the LLM code-navigation revolution. As they evolve, they'll become even more adept at understanding complex code structures and relationships, making your coding journey a breeze. So, ditch the confusion and embrace the power of LLMs - the code jungle awaits your exploration with newfound clarity!

8.3. Documentation Generation: From Code Chaos to Crystal Clarity

Imagine inheriting a codebase with cryptic functions and zero documentation – deciphering it feels like translating ancient hieroglyphics. Fear not, knowledge-hungry developer! LLMs (Large Language Models) are here to be your Rosetta Stone, **automatically generating clear, concise documentation** from your code itself.

Think of it as having a magic decoder ring for your code. Simply provide the code, and the LLM analyzes its structure, functionality, and purpose, then translates it into human-readable text. No more struggling to understand what each line does or spending hours writing documentation yourself.

But LLMs go beyond basic summaries. They can generate:

- **Comprehensive overviews:** Get a high-level understanding of your code's purpose, key features, and overall architecture.
- **Detailed function explanations:** Dive into individual functions, understanding their parameters, return values, and internal logic.
- **API reference guides:** Easily discover how to use your code's functions with clear explanations and usage examples.

Here are some real-world examples:

- **Open-source libraries:** Contribute to open-source projects by generating documentation for new features or bug fixes, making the code more accessible to others.
- **Internal codebases:** Improve team collaboration and knowledge sharing by automatically generating documentation for internal libraries or tools.
- **Personal projects:** Keep your own projects well-documented for future reference or potential sharing, ensuring you always understand your code's inner workings.

Ready to experience the documentation magic? Here's some code to get you started (using Bard):

Python

```python
# Install and set up Bard

# ...


# Provide your code snippet or file path

your_code = """
def calculate_area(length, width):

    """Calculates the area of a rectangle."""

  return length * width
```

```python
"""

# Generate documentation using Bard

documentation = Bard.generate_text(

    model="code-documentation",

    prompt=f"Generate documentation for the
following Python code:\n{your_code}",

    max_tokens=256,

    temperature=0.7,

)


# Print the generated documentation

print(documentation)
```

Remember, this is just the beginning. As LLMs evolve, their documentation generation capabilities will become even more sophisticated, even incorporating code examples, diagrams, and interactive elements. So, ditch the documentation dread and embrace the power of LLMs – let your code speak for itself with crystal clarity!

8.4. Chatbots and Virtual Assistants: From Robotic Responses to Real Conversations

Imagine this: you create a customer service chatbot, but instead of helpful interactions, it delivers robotic responses that leave users frustrated. Fear not, tech innovator! LLMs (Large Language Models) are here to be your conversation architects, crafting **intelligent chatbots and virtual assistants that understand natural language and respond in an engaging way**.

Think of it like having a superpowered dialogue engine. Instead of scripting rigid responses, you describe desired conversation flows, and the LLM builds chatbots that can hold meaningful conversations, answer questions accurately, and even adapt to different user intents and emotions.

But LLMs don't stop at basic chat. They can:

- **Personalize interactions:** Craft unique responses based on user context and history, creating a more natural and engaging experience.
- **Learn and adapt:** Continuously improve through interaction, refining responses and understanding new topics over time.

- **Handle complex requests:** Answer open-ended questions, complete tasks, and even troubleshoot issues, reducing the need for human intervention.

Here are some real-world examples:

- **Customer service:** Build chatbots that answer product inquiries, resolve issues, and even personalize recommendations, boosting customer satisfaction and reducing support costs.
- **Education:** Create AI tutors that answer student questions, provide feedback, and adapt to individual learning styles, personalizing the learning experience.
- **Entertainment:** Design chatbots for games or virtual worlds that engage users in conversations, creating more immersive and interactive experiences.

Ready to bring your chatbot to life? Here's some code to get you started (using Rasa):

Python

```python
# Install and set up Rasa

# ...


# Define your chatbot's intents (user goals) and entities (specific information)

intents = [
```

```
        {"name":  "greet",  "examples":
["hello", "hi"]},

     {"name": "order_pizza", "examples":
["order a pizza", "can I get a pizza"]}

]

entities = [

        {"name":  "pizza_size",  "values":
["small", "medium", "large"]}

]



# Train your chatbot using conversation
data (text and labels)

# ...



# Deploy your chatbot and let it start
interacting with users!

# ...
```

Remember, this is just a glimpse into the potential of LLMs for chatbot development. As these models evolve, they'll become even more adept at understanding human language nuances and generating contextually relevant responses, making your chatbots feel more like real conversations and less like robotic interactions. So, ditch the script and embrace the power of LLMs – let your chatbots engage users in truly human-like conversations!

P.S. Stay tuned for the final chapter, where we'll explore the vast possibilities of LLMs beyond coding, from creative writing to scientific discovery, and get a glimpse into the exciting future powered by these remarkable language models!

8.5. Beyond Code: Unveiling the LLM Universe

We've explored how LLMs (Large Language Models) can turbocharge your coding, but buckle up, because their potential goes far beyond lines of code. Get ready to unlock a universe of exciting applications that will transform various aspects of our lives!

1. Personalized Learning: Imagine an AI tutor that adapts to your learning style, answers your questions in natural language, and even creates personalized study plans. LLMs can make this a reality, revolutionizing education by providing tailored learning experiences for everyone.

Example: You're struggling with a complex math concept. Instead of dry textbooks, your LLM tutor explains it in an engaging way, provides interactive exercises, and adjusts its teaching based on your understanding.

2. Content Creation on Demand: Need a catchy marketing slogan, a captivating poem, or even a script for your next YouTube video? LLMs can be your creative partner, generating different content variations based on your style and specifications.

Example: You're writing a blog post about sustainable living. You give the LLM some keywords and your desired tone, and it generates several draft intros, helping you find the perfect starting point.

3. Data Analysis Unleashed: Sifting through massive datasets can be overwhelming. LLMs can analyze mountains of data, identify hidden patterns, and even summarize key insights in clear, human-readable language.

Example: You're analyzing customer feedback from social media. The LLM helps you categorize the sentiment, identify recurring themes, and even suggest potential areas for improvement.

4. Science, Reimagined: From generating hypotheses to analyzing research papers, LLMs are assisting scientists in pushing the boundaries of discovery. They can even help write scientific reports and explain complex concepts to a wider audience.

Example: You're researching a new material for solar panels. The LLM helps you analyze existing research, suggest promising avenues for exploration, and even write draft reports summarizing your findings.

5. The Future is Accessible: Imagine technology that seamlessly understands and responds to your natural language, regardless of disability or language barriers. LLMs are paving the way for more inclusive technology, like sign language translation tools and voice-controlled interfaces.

Example: You have limited mobility and rely on voice commands. Your LLM assistant understands your natural speech patterns and helps you control your smart home, access information, and connect with others.

Remember, this is just a taste of the possibilities. As LLMs continue to evolve, they'll become even more sophisticated, pushing the boundaries of what's possible in various fields. So, get ready to witness the incredible impact of LLMs shaping a future filled with personalized learning, creative expression, groundbreaking discoveries, and inclusive technology for all!

P.S. Stay curious, keep exploring, and let's embrace the exciting future powered by the potential of LLMs!

CHAPTER 9

Unleashing the Full Potential of Your Fine-tuned Models

Congratulations! You've built a fine-tuned LLM (Large Language Model) – a powerful tool ready to tackle your specific tasks. But the journey doesn't end there. Just like a master sculptor refines their art, **evaluating and optimizing** your LLM is crucial to unlock its true potential. Buckle up, because we're about to delve into the exciting world of metrics, analysis, and iterative improvement!

9.1. Selecting the Right Metrics: Choosing Your Measuring Stick for Success

Imagine baking a cake: its final form isn't enough to judge its quality. You'd taste it, check its texture, and ensure it matches your recipe's expectations. Evaluating your fine-tuned LLM (Large Language Model) follows the same principle. Choosing the right **metrics** acts as your evaluation tools, revealing how well your LLM performs and guiding you towards optimization.

But with a plethora of metrics available, which ones should you choose? It all hinges on your **goals**. Are you building a chatbot that needs to understand user intent with laser focus? **Accuracy metrics** like F1 score will be your compass. Crafting a content generator that spins creative, engaging text? Then **fluency and coherence scores** become your North Star. Remember, **relevance is paramount**. Don't get swayed by fancy metrics that don't resonate with your LLM's purpose.

Let's illustrate this with some real-world examples:

1. Building a Question-Answering System:

Here, you'd focus on metrics like:

- **Accuracy:** The percentage of questions your LLM answers correctly. This is a crucial starting point, but remember, accuracy doesn't tell the whole story.
- **BLEU score:** This measures how well your LLM's answers match the expected format and phrasing of the correct answer. For example, if the answer should be a factual statement, your LLM shouldn't respond with a question or an opinion.

Here's some code to calculate BLEU score in Python using the nltk library:

Python

```python
from nltk.translate.bleu_score import sentence_bleu
```

```python
# Your generated answer

generated_answer = "The capital of France
is Paris."

# The expected answer (gold standard)

reference_answer = "Paris is the capital
of France."


# Calculate BLEU score

bleu_score                              =
sentence_bleu(reference_answer.split(),
generated_answer.split())


print(f"BLEU score: {bleu_score}")
```

2. Fine-tuning a Sentiment Analysis Model:

Here, your focus shifts to metrics like:

- **Precision:** This measures the percentage of positive/negative/neutral classifications that were actually correct. For example, if your LLM classifies a review as "positive" and it truly is, that's a precise prediction.
- **Recall:** This measures how well your LLM identifies all the actual positive/negative/neutral reviews. For example, if there are 100 truly positive reviews, and your LLM identifies 80 of them, its recall is 80%.
- **F1 score:** This combines precision and recall into a single metric, giving you a balanced view of your model's performance.

Here's some code to calculate F1 score in Python using scikit-learn:

Python

```python
from sklearn.metrics import f1_score



# True sentiment labels for your data

true_labels = [1, 0, 2, ...]   # 1 for
positive, 0 for negative, 2 for neutral

# Predicted sentiment labels by your LLM

predicted_labels = [1, 2, 1, ...]
```

```python
# Calculate F1 score for each sentiment
class and overall F1 score

f1_scores      =       f1_score(true_labels,
predicted_labels, average=None)

overall_f1_score = f1_score(true_labels,
predicted_labels, average='weighted')


print(f"F1   scores   for   each   sentiment
class: {f1_scores}")

print(f"Overall           F1           score:
{overall_f1_score}")
```

Remember, these are just starting points. **Metrics are valuable tools, but they're just the beginning.** In the next section, we'll delve into the art of analyzing your results and identifying areas for improvement, helping you refine your LLM and unlock its full potential!

9.2. Analyzing Results and Identifying Improvement Opportunities: Cracking the Code on Your LLM's Performance

Imagine baking a cake: sure, it looks golden brown on top, but is it perfectly cooked inside? Evaluating your fine-tuned LLM goes beyond a surface check. **Analyzing results** is where the real magic happens, helping you identify areas for improvement and refine your model into a champion performer. Metrics provide valuable clues, but they're just the starting point. You, the data detective, must **piece together the evidence and uncover the deeper story**. Here's your toolkit:

1. Become an Error Inspector: Don't just shrug off incorrect outputs. **Investigate!**

- **Analyze error patterns:** Are certain types of queries constantly tripping up your LLM? Are there specific grammatical structures causing problems? Group errors by category to identify recurring weaknesses.
- **Code example:** Let's say your sentiment analysis model keeps misclassifying sarcastic reviews as positive. Use libraries like pandas to group errors based on sentiment and review text.

Python

```python
import pandas as pd


# Load your error data

errors = pd.DataFrame({'text': ["I loved
this movie!", "It was the worst movie ever
(sarcastic)"],      'predicted_sentiment':
['positive',               'positive'],
```

```python
'true_sentiment':                    ['positive',
'negative']})
```

```python
# Group errors by predicted sentiment and
analyze text patterns
```

```python
positive_errors                              =
errors[errors['predicted_sentiment']    ==
'positive']
```

```python
for text in positive_errors['text']:

    # Look for common elements like
exclamation    marks,    parentheses,    or
specific  phrases  that  might  indicate
sarcasm

    print(text)    # Analyze each text
manually to identify patterns
```

- **Refine your training data:** Based on your analysis, add more nuanced examples to your training data. For the sarcasm example, include movie reviews with clear sarcastic language and their corresponding negative sentiment labels.

2. Embrace Performance Diversification: Put your LLM to the test on diverse inputs. **How does it perform on different tasks or data subsets?**

- **Compare performance across tasks:** Test your LLM on different tasks within your domain. For example, if you have a chatbot, test its question-answering, summarization, and dialogue generation capabilities.
- **Code example:** Imagine you have a chatbot for customer service. Use different datasets for factual questions (e.g., "What are your store hours?") and open-ended inquiries (e.g., "I'm having trouble with my order"). Analyze accuracy and fluency metrics for each task.
- **Identify performance variations:** Look for differences in performance across data subsets. This might reveal biases or limitations in your model.
- **Code example:** If your LLM performs poorly on reviews containing informal language, analyze its performance on formal and informal datasets separately. This could indicate a need for more diverse training data.

3. Visualization is Key: Don't get bogged down in numbers. **Visualize your metrics!**

- **Confusion matrices:** These reveal which classes your LLM struggles to differentiate. For example, a confusion matrix for sentiment analysis might show it often confuses "neutral" and "positive" reviews.

- **Code example:** Use libraries like scikit-plot to create confusion matrices.

Python

```
from        scikitplot.metrics        import
plot_confusion_matrix



# Calculate confusion matrix for your
sentiment analysis model

plot_confusion_matrix(true_labels,
predicted_labels)
```

- **Attention maps:** These highlight the parts of the input your LLM focuses on during decision-making. For example, an attention map for text summarization might show it focusing more on irrelevant details instead of key points.
- **Code example:** Use libraries like transformers to generate attention maps for your specific LLM architecture.

4. Context is King: Don't analyze results in isolation. **Consider the context of your LLM's purpose and target audience.**

- **Tailor error analysis:** What might be a minor error in one context could be critical in another. For example, a grammatical mistake in a customer service chatbot could be perceived as unprofessional, while it might be acceptable in a creative writing tool.
- **Code example:** During error analysis, consider the specific context of each error (e.g., task, target audience) and prioritize improvements based on potential impact.

Remember, analyzing results is an iterative journey. As you identify weaknesses, you can refine your training data, adjust hyperparameters, or even explore different LLM architectures. Each iteration brings you closer to a model that truly shines at your specific tasks.

P.S. Stay tuned for the next section, where we'll delve into the exciting world of fine-tuning further, exploring advanced techniques and tools to take your LLM to the next level!

9.3. Fine-tuning Further: Sculpting Your LLM into a Masterpiece

Imagine meticulously shaping a block of marble, revealing the hidden masterpiece within. Fine-tuning your LLM (Large Language Model) is similar – each iteration brings it closer to its full potential. Now, armed with insights from analyzing results, let's explore advanced techniques to **optimize further**:

1. Data Do-Over: Building a Strong Foundation

The foundation of any great model is its **training data**. Based on your analysis, consider these refinements:

- **Add more data:** If your LLM struggles with specific types of input, expand your training data with more diverse examples.

Example: Your sentiment analysis model misclassified sarcastic reviews. Expand your data with movie reviews labeled as "sarcastic positive" and "sarcastic negative" to teach it the nuances of sarcasm.

- **Improve data quality:** Ensure your data is accurate, representative, and free of biases. Clean and pre-process your data thoroughly.

Example: Remove typos and inconsistencies from your customer service chatbot training data to avoid biased or nonsensical responses.

- **Data augmentation:** Creatively manipulate existing data to artificially increase its volume and diversity.

Code example (using Python libraries nltk **and** random**):**

Python

```python
from nltk.corpus import wordnet

from random import choice


def synonym_replacement(text):

  synonyms = []
```

```
for word in text.split():

    for syn in wordnet.synsets(word):

        for lemma in syn.lemmas():

            synonyms.append(lemma.name())

    random_synonym = choice(synonyms)

        return    text.replace(random_synonym,
choice(synonyms))


# Augment your training data with synonyms

augmented_data                            =
[synonym_replacement(sentence)            for
sentence in your_data]
```

2. Hyperparameter Tuning: Dialing for Excellence

These are the dials and levers that control your LLM's learning process. Experiment with adjusting them to see how they impact performance:

- **Learning rate:** This controls how quickly the model updates its internal parameters based on new information.

Code example (using TensorFlow):

Python

```
model = tf.keras.Sequential(...)    # Your
LLM architecture



# Experiment with different learning rates

optimizer                                =
tf.keras.optimizers.Adam(learning_rate=0.0
01)   # Initial learning rate

model.compile(optimizer=optimizer,
loss='categorical_crossentropy',
metrics=['accuracy'])

model.fit(X_train, y_train, epochs=10)



# Try a lower learning rate for finer
adjustments
```

```
optimizer                                    =
tf.keras.optimizers.Adam(learning_rate=0.0
001)

model.compile(optimizer=optimizer,
loss='categorical_crossentropy',
metrics=['accuracy'])

model.fit(X_train, y_train, epochs=10)
```

- **Batch size:** This determines how many training examples the model sees at once before updating its parameters.

3. Advanced Architectures: Pushing the Boundaries

If your basic fine-tuning hasn't yielded the desired results, consider exploring more sophisticated LLM architectures:

- **Transfer learning:** Leverage a pre-trained LLM on a massive dataset and fine-tune it on your specific task.

Code example (using Transformers library):

Python

```
from          transformers          import
AutoModelForSequenceClassification,
AutoTokenizer
```

```python
# Load pre-trained T5 model for text
summarization

model_name = "t5-base"

tokenizer                             =
AutoTokenizer.from_pretrained(model_name)

model                                 =
AutoModelForSequenceClassification.from_pr
etrained(model_name,   num_labels=1)    #
Adjust num_labels for your task



# Fine-tune on your summarization dataset

# ...
```

- **Ensemble methods:** Combine predictions from multiple LLMs to create a more robust and accurate model.

Code example (using scikit-learn):

```
Python

from        sklearn.ensemble        import
VotingClassifier
```

```python
# Train multiple LLMs with different
hyperparameters

models = [..., ...]  # Your trained LLM
models


# Combine predictions using voting

ensemble                              =
VotingClassifier(estimators=models,
voting='hard')

ensemble.fit(X_train, y_train)

predictions = ensemble.predict(X_test)
```

Remember, fine-tuning is an iterative process. Experiment, analyze, and refine. Each step takes you closer to a truly exceptional LLM, tailored to your specific needs.

P.S. Stay tuned for the final chapter, where we'll explore the vast possibilities of LLMs beyond coding, from creative writing to scientific discovery, and get a glimpse into the exciting future powered by

Conclusion

So Long, and Thanks for All the LLMs!

Whew, folks! We've navigated the thrilling terrain of fine-tuning LLMs, from the basic building blocks to advanced optimization tips. You've learned how to sculpt these language models into mighty tools, ready to tackle your specific needs. But remember, this is just the prologue in a much grander narrative.

Think of LLMs as your artistic collaborators, constantly evolving and eager to shatter the boundaries of what's possible. They're not just code-wielding robots; they can be storytellers, poets, even scientists! Imagine an LLM composing a symphony that rivals Mozart's, or crafting a poem that captures the human soul with stunning depth. Or picture it generating groundbreaking scientific theories that unlock the universe's mysteries.

The potential is infinite, and you, the LLM sculptor, hold the chisel. As you continue to experiment, refine, and push the limits, you're not just creating powerful tools – you're shaping the future of language, creativity, and innovation. So, keep exploring, keep learning, and keep fine-tuning. The most astonishing chapters of this story are yet to be written, and you have the pen in your hand.

You made it!

You've navigated the intricate world of fine-tuning LLMs and emerged victorious! I'm truly impressed by your dedication and eager to see the incredible software you'll build with this newfound knowledge.

If this journey has been valuable, I'd be incredibly grateful if you could consider leaving a review on your preferred platform. Your honest feedback not only helps me refine future content but also empowers others embarking on their LLM exploration.

But your learning doesn't stop here! I've written several other books delving deeper into various aspects of artificial intelligence and its applications. Visit [insert your website or store link] to discover a treasure trove of resources and fuel your AI learning adventure.

Thank you once again for choosing this book. I truly appreciate you joining me on this journey, and I wish you all the best in your future endeavors!

Glossary of Key Terms and Concepts

Understanding LLMs: A Quick Reference Guide

This glossary breaks down key terms and concepts related to Large Language Models (LLMs) in simple, straightforward language. Think of it like your cheat sheet for navigating the world of LLMs!

A. LLM Basics:

- **Large Language Model (LLM):** Imagine a super-powered language learner, trained on massive amounts of text. LLMs understand and generate human-like language, tackling tasks like writing, translating, and answering questions.
- **Fine-tuning:** Picture customizing your LLM for a specific job. By giving it relevant data, you train it to excel in your area, like understanding medical texts or writing catchy ad copy.
- **Metrics:** These are like report cards for your LLM, measuring how well it performs its tasks. Think accuracy, precision, and other fancy terms that basically tell you if it's doing what you need it to do.
- **Hyperparameters:** These are the controls under the hood of your LLM. Adjusting them, like changing the learning speed, can impact how well it learns and performs.
- **Data Augmentation:** Imagine expanding your LLM's knowledge by making up new examples. This helps it learn broader concepts and perform even better.

B. What LLMs Can Do:

- **Question Answering:** Stumped by something? Ask your LLM! It can search through mountains of information and deliver answers in a clear, informative way.
- **Text Summarization:** Need the gist of a long article? No problem! Your LLM can condense it into a shorter, key-point-filled summary.
- **Machine Translation:** Speaking different languages is a breeze for LLMs. They can translate text from one language to another, breaking down communication barriers.
- **Dialogue Generation:** Chatbots powered by LLMs can have natural conversations, answering questions and providing information just like a real person.
- **Content Creation:** Feeling uninspired? Let your LLM spark your creativity! It can write poems, scripts, even code based on your prompts and desired styles.

C. LLM Tech Talk (Simplified):

- **Tokenization:** Think of it like chopping text into bite-sized pieces (words, parts of words). This helps the LLM understand and process information.
- **Transformer:** Imagine a complex network of connections that helps the LLM understand relationships between words in a sentence. It's like a super brain for language!
- **Attention Mechanism:** Picture the LLM focusing its spotlight on specific parts of the text it's processing. This

helps it understand the meaning and context more accurately.

- **Pre-trained Model:** Think of it as an LLM with a head start. It's already learned a lot from massive datasets, and you can fine-tune it for your specific needs.

D. Examples and Code (Python):

1. Tokenization:

Python

```python
# Splitting a sentence into words
from nltk.tokenize import word_tokenize

text = "This is an example sentence."
words = word_tokenize(text)
print(words)    # Output: ['This', 'is', 'an', 'example', 'sentence']
```

2. Attention Mechanism (Simplified):

Python

```python
# Imagine using an LLM with attention (e.g., BERT)

# Process text and access attention weights
```

```
attention_weights = analyze_text(text)


# Visualize the weights to see which parts of the text
received more focus

visualize_attention(attention_weights)
```

Remember, this is just the beginning! The world of LLMs is constantly evolving, with new terms and concepts popping up all the time. Keep exploring and learning to stay ahead of the curve!

Community Resources and Further Exploration: Deepen Your LLM Journey

Whether you're a budding LLM enthusiast or a seasoned developer, delving deeper into this exciting field brings immense value. This section provides key resources and pathways to expand your knowledge and exploration.

A. Community Hubs:

- **Forums and Discussion Boards:** Engage with fellow LLM users and developers on platforms like Reddit's r/languagemodels, Hugging Face forums, or the TensorFlow Discuss board. Share experiences, ask questions, and learn from diverse perspectives.
- **Social Media Groups:** Connect with like-minded individuals on groups like the Large Language Model Alliance on LinkedIn or relevant Facebook groups. Participate in discussions, stay updated on advancements, and network with potential collaborators.

B. Educational Resources:

- **Online Courses and Tutorials:** Platforms like Coursera, edX, and Udacity offer various LLM-related courses, from introductory overviews to specialized topics like fine-tuning or ethical considerations. Choose a course that aligns with your skill level and interests.
- **Blogs and Articles:** Renowned organizations and researchers like OpenAI, Hugging Face, and Google AI

regularly publish insightful blog posts and articles covering LLM developments, best practices, and applications. Stay informed and learn from the experts.

C. Experimentation Platforms:

- **Colab and Kaggle Notebooks:** Leverage these interactive platforms to experiment with pre-trained LLMs, explore code examples, and fine-tune models for specific tasks. Collaborate with others and share your findings, fostering a culture of open exploration.
- **LLM APIs and Cloud Services:** Numerous providers offer access to pre-trained LLMs through APIs or cloud services, allowing you to integrate their capabilities into your applications without extensive infrastructure setup. Experiment with different models and functionalities to discover the best fit for your needs.

D. Deeper Dives:

- **Research Papers and Publications:** As you delve deeper, explore published research papers on specific LLM architectures, fine-tuning techniques, and various applications. Start with well-cited and accessible papers to build a strong foundation before venturing into more complex topics.
- **Conferences and Workshops:** Attend specialized conferences and workshops dedicated to LLMs. Immerse yourself in the latest advancements, network with leading researchers and practitioners, and gain valuable insights from presentations and discussions.

Remember: This is just a starting point. As the LLM field rapidly evolves, stay curious, explore new resources, and actively engage with the community. By combining formal learning, experimentation, and community engagement, you'll continuously expand your knowledge and contribute to the exciting future of LLMs!

Key Terms and Concepts:

- **LLM:** Large Language Model - A powerful AI model trained on massive text data, capable of understanding and generating human-like language.
- **Fine-tuning:** Adapting a pre-trained LLM to a specific task or domain by further training it on relevant data.
- **API:** Application Programming Interface - A set of instructions that allows different software components to communicate with each other.
- **Cloud Service:** A service that provides access to computing resources over the internet, typically on a pay-as-you-go basis.

I hope this information empowers you to continue your LLM journey with confidence!

www.ingramcontent.com/pod-product-compliance
Lightning Source LLC
LaVergne TN
LVHW051735050326
832903LV00023B/932